THE COMMUNITY
NEEDS ASSESSMENT
WORKBOOK

Related books of interest

THE COMMUNITY NEEDS ASSESSMENT WORKBOOK

Rodney A. Wambeam

University of Wyoming

LYCEUM
BOOKS, INC.

Chicago, Illinois

Published by
LYCEUM BOOKS, INC.
5758 S. Blackstone Avenue
Chicago, Illinois 60637
773-643-1903 fax
773-643-1902 phone
lyceum@lyceumbooks.com
www.lyceumbooks.com

6 5 4 3 2 1   14 15 16 17 18

ISBN 978-1-935871-53-8

Printed in the United States of America.

Library of Congress Cataloging-in-Publication Data pending.

To learn more about applied community research and to download the worksheets
and tools in this book, visit rodneywambeam.com.

To Laurie Homer,
the perfect wife, and my best friend
for more than thirty years

Contents

Preface   ix
Acknowledgments   xiii

Step 1   PLANNING YOUR NEEDS ASSESSMENT   1
   Chapter 1   Introduction   3
   Chapter 2   Laying the Foundation   9

Step 2   COLLECTING AND ANALYZING DATA   21
   Chapter 3   Types of Data   23
   Chapter 4   Collecting Qualitative Data   51
   Chapter 5   Collecting Quantitative Data   91
   Chapter 6   Analyzing Qualitative Data   131
   Chapter 7   Analyzing Quantitative Data   151

Step 3   FINALIZING AND USING YOUR
         NEEDS ASSESSMENT   189
   Chapter 8   Answering Research Questions and
           Setting Priorities 191
   Chapter 9   Writing the Technical Report   201
   Chapter 10 Using a Comprehensive Needs Assessment   219

References   233
Index   237

Preface

Needs assessments are most important as the first step in social and strategic planning. Occasionally, this begins by creating a "statement of need" in a grant application. I have written these for multimillion dollar federal projects and small thousand-dollar local efforts. The goal of a statement of need is to show that services are required and the community has a problem. This type of needs assessment stems from grant proposals asking us to prove we need the funding, so we walk the fine line between describing how bad our problem is and how great we could be at solving it, with just a little more money. These sections of an application bring out the best in my creative writing. I once started the needs statement for a small foundation grant to provide new skates for a local ice speed skating team with this sentence, "At 7,200 feet winters are long and opportunities are limited." On another occasion I was able to play up local culture while making my point.

> The rural population, pioneer history, frontier spirit, natural beauty, and often harsh climate of Wyoming and Weston County combine to create a culture of libertarian independence. While Weston County is a wonderful place to live, this culture can have consequences. Most common is the misperception that underage drinking is a safe rite of passage and binge drinking is just a cowboy "holding his liquor." As a result, Weston County youth binge drink at very high rates.

I have also facilitated the determination of need at a community level in order to fully understand the social issues of greatest importance. This involved everything from school-based surveys to sorting through mountains of data to make sense of local problems. On one occasion I helped a sexual violence prevention planning committee complete a needs assessment by looking at school data, crime data, and other relevant sources. We found, while the public fears sexual predators jumping out of bushes and attacking children, most victims knew their attacker. And most attackers were other children. Indeed, 14 percent of ninth- through twelfth-grade girls and 8 percent of ninth- through twelfth-grade boys in this community had been forced to have intercourse against their will. These findings helped the committee choose appropriate strategies to combat sexual violence specific to local schools. On another occasion I worked with a coordinated health care group to prioritize a variety of data indicators by creating data profiles and a structure for comparing unrelated facts and figures. The group was driven by too few resources and too many problems. The needs assessment enabled them to make decisions about funding allocation to their disparate membership. Both types of needs assessment described above have in common a desire to make data-driven decisions—to base social services upon something other than what "feels right" or "the way we have always done it."

In 2005 I became the lead evaluator of a major federally funded substance abuse prevention project in my home state of Wyoming. This project required the completion of a comprehensive statewide needs assessment by the newly created State Epidemiological Workgroup. I facilitated this workgroup, and my staff and I served as the labor force that collected, analyzed, and reported the findings from this important research project. Our federal partners advised us to consider only a subset of the most important data sources to keep the needs assessment manageable; we, of course, did the opposite. The workgroup considered the universe of data sources (86 of them) and the universe of indicators from these sources (269 of them) having anything to do with substance abuse in Wyoming. The resulting analysis and prioritization of data was daunting, yet the workgroup ably identified a small set of problems for Wyoming's prevention system to target. The comprehensive statewide needs assessment sought to prioritize a substance abuse problem for a massive federally funded project, and later drove the creation of a needs assessment workbook for Wyoming's prevention communities. This latter workbook led to a remarkable set of community documents, and in turn, to the community needs assessment workbook you hold in your hands.

We based the project itself upon a strategic planning model (described in more detail in chapter 1). Wyoming not only began with a state-level needs assessment, but every funded sub-recipient community also started with a needs assessment. The state needs assessment described above had already prioritized the problem that communities must target. We created the community needs assessment workbook to document the targeted problems in communities and to identify and prioritize the causes of those problems. The workbook served two purposes. First, it provided communities with a practical and logical approach to determining their needs. Using this prioritization method, they were able to better choose social service strategies. Second, it helped build local capacity for understanding and using data. By all accounts the workbook was a success in Wyoming and has been adapted on numerous occasions by other states and communities as well as for other social issues.

For these reasons, I decided to write this book as a way to help all communities collect, analyze, and prioritize local data in a simple and logical way. The goal is to build your capacity to work with data while completing a sound community needs assessment. The product of your work can be used when writing a funding proposal or when using the best possible data to plan social service delivery. I do not intend this book to be simply a text on how to conduct a needs assessment; rather, it serves as a step-by-step guide to completing a real needs assessment. It differs from other needs assessment texts in its focus on actually creating a comprehensive community needs assessment as you read. It contains numerous tasks, worksheets, demonstrations, exercises, and tools to aid the reader in completing the research project. In short, it is called a workbook because I expect you to create products while you learn. In the end, I hope this book rewards you with a useful document to guide your community efforts.

The primary audience for this book is professionals who provide social services and participate in community organizing. They can use this book to conduct an actual and useful comprehensive community needs assessment. Secondarily, college students in a variety of social service disciplines from counseling and social work to health sciences and criminal justice will find this a useful guide when preparing for a career helping people and communities. Classes can make use of the workbook style to teach the needs assessment process, and individuals can utilize the workbook itself to complete larger projects like a senior thesis. I envision a world where all helping organizations and groups of caring individuals make decisions based upon solid information about their communities. The result would be a world where social service providers are more effective and efficient, and ultimately communities are better off because of it.

The work itself is broken into three steps. Step 1 details a process for planning your needs assessment and includes an introductory chapter and a chapter on creating your workgroup, describing your community, and defining your research questions. The purpose of this step is to build a strong foundation for your needs assessment work. Step 2 leads you through the gathering and breakdown of data. It includes chapters on types of data, collecting and analyzing qualitative data, and collecting and analyzing quantitative data. The final outcomes of this step include generalizations and discoveries to help answer your research questions and make data-driven decisions. Step 3 helps you finalize the needs assessment. It includes chapters on answering your research questions, writing a technical report, and putting the results to good use. The purpose of this step is to use the needs assessment to inform and support the other steps of the strategic planning model. When you are done with all of this work, you will have valuable products and the knowledge to gather and analyze data as part of a community-based needs assessment.

Acknowledgments

Much like a needs assessment final report, a book may have a single author but is the work of many individuals. I would like to acknowledge the contributions of the numerous people who made this book possible. My many friends and colleagues at the Wyoming Survey and Analysis Center teach me something new on a weekly basis and make it fun to come to work. Eric Canen and Kay Lang worked with me on the original community needs assessment workbook in Wyoming, and inspire me with their hard work, dedication, and creativity. Trena Anastasia introduced me to her friends at Lyceum Books and in turn listened to my writing troubles like only a good friend can. Of course, David Follmer and everyone at Lyceum kept on top of me to complete the manuscript on time and in publishable condition. Night Heron Books always had warm coffee and a place to sit while I worked. Novelist Ben Tanzer, a much better writer than I, allowed me to continuously bother him with updates and questions. Writers understand how important a sympathetic listener can be. My young friend Ali Briere provided a thorough edit the way only a grammar-obsessed student can. My wife Laurie Homer, who is a terrific writer and social service provider, gave me honest feedback and insight. My children waited many Sunday mornings for their daddy to finish working on his book and come home to make breakfast in bed. Finally, everything that appears in this book is possible because of the countless government agencies, as well as large and small communities, that gave me the chance to research with and for them. I am forever in their debt for that opportunity.

PLANNING YOUR
NEEDS ASSESSMENT

Step 1 of this workbook details a process for planning your needs assessment. It includes an introductory chapter and a chapter on creating the foundation of your research. You will gain an understanding of the purpose of completing a local needs assessment, how it relates to a strategic planning model, and how this model and completion of this needs assessment will improve your work in the helping professions. By the end of step 1, you will also create three specific products. The first is your definition of community. The second is a needs assessment workgroup whose membership includes community members who possess necessary data, represent relevant and diverse populations, and have the power to make decisions. The third is detailed research questions that drive your community needs assessment.

THE LEARNING TAKEAWAYS FOR STEP 1 INCLUDE:

- The definition and purpose of needs assessment research
- How to define your community and use that definition to shape your needs assessment
- How to develop a needs assessment workgroup
- How to create detailed research questions

Introduction

Perceptions of need come from many sources. News reports, television crime dramas, the latest Internet fad, cultural norms, political interest groups, shocking local events, and published research studies may all contribute to our perception of need around social issues. Several years ago, I was working as a prevention researcher in Nebraska when a teenage girl was found frozen to death in a cornfield after using jimson weed (sometimes known as gypsum, devil's, Jamestown, or loco weed) to get high. It caused an uproar in the small town where it happened and across the state. Immediately substance abuse prevention efforts turned to the problem of jimson weed, but few people involved in this speedy response stopped to consider if this was an isolated incident or a true public health epidemic. Had jimson weed surpassed alcohol and tobacco as the biggest source of substance abuse-related problems in the community? Do other youth use jimson weed? How did this girl know to use jimson weed to get high? Does it grow in Nebraska or did it come from somewhere else? If it does grow in Nebraska, are efforts in place to eradicate the weed? Answering questions like these separates perception of need—or misperception of need—from a true understanding of community problems and the necessity for social service solutions. The best way to achieve this understanding is through a systematic analysis of community data. A needs assessment provides this, and it is my hope this workbook will give you the necessary tools to do a quality job of answering the questions of need that arise in your community.

While the term *needs assessment* was first used in the 1960s, it has more recently become commonplace among social service providers and a legitimate form of social science research. Social service providers generally use needs assessments to discover the magnitude and seriousness of problems and to make data-driven decisions about service delivery. The purpose of a needs assessment is to create useful and objective information. However, need is a concept with multiple meanings. Posavac and Carey (2011) argue the assessment of need is generally an exercise in measuring the "discrepancy between what is and what should be" (p. 109). Others have detailed this discrepancy as between an actual state and an ideal, a normal, a minimum, a desired, or an expected state (Roth, 1990). Need has also been defined as what people or a community must have to be in a satisfactory state (Scriven & Roth, 1990). The latter definition illustrates the difference between understanding the gap between what is and what should be and what is needed to close this gap.

A good needs assessment should point the way to possible solutions to community problems. In the preface, I mentioned a needs assessment that identified sexual violence in schools as a crisis. Roughly 14 percent of ninth- through twelfth-grade girls in this community had been forced to have intercourse against their will. Data from the Youth Risk Behavior Survey provided this description of a problem that is likely underreported. The needs assessment workgroup identified this problem as anything but ideal or desired. Indeed, they believed a satisfactory state would be one where no high school girl was ever forced to have intercourse against her will. However, they took the next step to detail the current lack of programs and policies in schools to address the issue. Health classes failed to teach positive sexual relationships, and many schools ignored a culture that promoted sexual violence among students. The workgroup used this information to make recommendations on where to focus sexual violence prevention efforts and what strategies might effectively address the problem. This example shows that how our needs assessment defines and describes a problem influences the possible social solutions to that problem.

Note that, while the data collected and analyzed in a needs assessment may be unbiased and exact, *need* is a relative term and values will be part of the process. Researchers must account for the interpretation of data and the political context of an assessment. In the above example, the sexual violence needs assessment workgroup recommended funding to specific schools for specific strategies. However, this recommendation did not include the one thing they believed most effective. Based upon past experiences, the workgroup wanted to recommend youth programming around healthy and appropriate sex lives, but they did not want to jeopardize their hard work by becoming the workgroup that promoted teenage sex. The best way to understand and account for values and political context is to form what Altschuld and Witkin (2000) call a needs assessment committee. I prefer the term *needs assessment workgroup* because you will expect this group of stakeholders to work hard on the project. Chapter 2 provides more details about selecting this workgroup. For now, know that the needs assessment workgroup plays a fundamental role in using and completing this workbook, and one of their primary jobs is to understand and account for values and political context.

A common strategic planning model for social services serves as the foundation for this workbook. It places needs assessment as the first of five very important steps in creating healthy communities, and social service providers can apply this model with great success. Figure 1 illustrates this simple process.

Figure 1 Strategic Planning Model

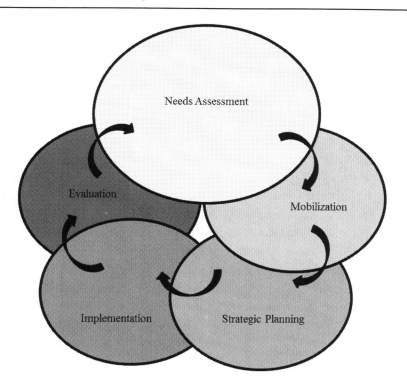

The process starts with a needs assessment that leads to the mobilization of stakeholders and creation of a data-driven strategic plan. Implementation and evaluation follow. While the model presents all five components as steps, practice shows that they often take place simultaneously. For example, the mobilization of stakeholders is a constant challenge in communities and evaluation must be considered from the outset not just at the end of any project. Moreover, the process is cyclical—meaning the final evaluation leads to further needs assessment, mobilization, planning, implementation, and ultimately more evaluation. Data drives this process, making the needs assessment of great importance. Objective and systematic needs assessment data mobilizes stakeholders and informs the strategic plan. It also lays the foundation for a rigorous evaluation. Needs assessment data provides the workgroup a baseline with which to make comparisons. I include the model here only to place needs assessment into the context of effective planning for the provision of services within your community.

Another component of healthy communities is an emphasis on a social ecological model that views change at numerous levels including individual, relationship, community, and societal (Bronfenbrenner & Morris, 1998). This workbook targets the community level and assumes you want to change neighborhoods, cultural groups, towns, counties, or states with your work. Mine is an epidemiological perspective that differs dramatically from an intervention perspective where human service workers provide one-on-one counseling, mentoring matches, or programs for youth. Intervention strategies should be part of a community change plan. However, entire communities are this workbook's unit of change. It is very valuable to answer questions like: What type of treatment do our clients need? Or how many children need after-school tutoring? But this workbook asks a much larger and often more complicated set of questions. How should our community spend its limited resources for social services? What specific problems should our coalition target? Or what community factors are causing our biggest and most serious problems? This workbook helps you identify and then answer questions like these in order to create community-level change.

In the upcoming chapters, you will encounter a number of accessories and activities to help you complete the initial step of the strategic planning model. First, each chapter contains specific tasks to be completed by you in coordination with your needs assessment workgroup. Second, this book is full of essential worksheets that, when completed, become the building blocks of your needs assessment. These worksheets vary from simple jobs like defining your community to more complicated jobs like writing survey questions. Third, I provide demonstrations that tell the stories of how people like you have completed important needs assessment tasks in their communities. These stories give you examples and hopefully confidence as you move forward with your own research. Fourth, exercises can be found in various chapters as a way for you to practice the necessary skills to create a high-quality research project. Finally, the workbook contains several indispensable research tools. These include a focus group protocol, a survey template, a sample parental consent form, and other potentially useful trappings of the social science profession. You can download the worksheets and tools found in this book for your own use by visiting rodneywambeam.com.

Chapter 2 represents the first step of your journey and helps you define your community, identify your needs assessment workgroup, and detail your research questions. Following its completion you will experience the initial joy of breathing fresh air and smelling the forest at the start of a good long hike—inasmuch as research can be compared to an exhilarating walk in the woods.

FURTHER READINGS

To learn more about the role of needs assessments or the needs assessment process as it relates to social services, consider reading one of the following texts. Each answers the question of why needs assessments are important and provides a discussion around the process of completing a needs assessment for social services.

Altschuld, J. W., & Witkin, B. R. (2000). *From needs assessment to action: Transforming needs into solution strategies*. Thousand Oaks, CA: Sage Publications.

Royse, D., Staton-Tindall, M., Badger, K., & Webster, M. J. (2009). *Needs assessment*. New York: Oxford University Press.

Soriano, F. I. (1995). *Conducting needs assessment: A multidisciplinary approach*. Thousand Oaks, CA: Sage Publications.

Laying the Foundation

Like any sturdy building, research projects must begin with a solid foundation. This chapter builds this foundation by helping you define your community, identify your needs assessment workgroup, and detail your research questions. Scientific inquiry (including a needs assessment) is driven by questions. I have had the misfortune of being part of research projects that lacked a distinct research question. In these cases, the research often becomes unmanageable, unfocused, and disorganized. One national multisite project evaluation created a community-level survey that over time became hundreds of pages long and included nearly every possible question a team of enthusiastic researchers could imagine. Their hope was to gather enough information and analyze enough data that they might find meaningful results, but they found little of use. Moreover, communities across the United States received only increased burden from a survey that took nearly two full days to complete every six months. On the other hand, I have benefited from being part of research projects driven by very specific research questions. One campus-based suicide prevention project used a simple three-question e-mail survey to gather valuable information from faculty, staff, and resident assistants to answer the basic but important question: did the implemented trainings increase the number of referrals of at-risk students? Once you outline your community, workgroup, and research questions your research will feel more manageable and organized.

TASK 1: DEFINE YOUR COMMUNITY

In order to change a community we need to understand that community. Community can be defined in various ways. Geography provides the most basic and common description of community. Eugene, Oregon, the Wind River Reservation in Wyoming, El Paso County, Texas, the SoHo neighborhood of New York City, and the state of Florida are all geographic communities—communities based upon location. The ability to draw these places on a map sets them apart. Other communities are harder to define. Some communities may be based upon organizations. Examples include the public schools of Denver, Colorado, or the members of the Actors' Equity Association, a labor union that represents actors and stage managers in the United States. Still other communities may be based upon culture. Communities of culture include religious, ethnic, and other demographic groups. Examples include the Native American population of Oklahoma, the elderly in America, or the transient homeless population that travel through any given city. Today, with the rise of social networking and our shrinking world, nebulous communities that may need social services even exist on the Internet.

With this in mind, your first task is to define the community you will study—be it geographic, organizational, or cultural. Worksheet 1 provides the framework for carrying out this task.

Completing worksheet 1 involves collecting specific numbers and a little creative writing. I include question 1a as an initial attempt to make you consider the community rather than the individuals you serve. Most needs assessments define community geographically, and question 1b requires you to define the actual location you will study if your community is geographic. This can be as simple as answering, "Our community is Ballard County, Kentucky." However, defining geographic communities may also involve the streets that border each side of an urban neighborhood or a river that separates one part of a city from another. When answering question 1b remember to include the size of your community. For example, how many square miles or city blocks does it cover? Answers to these questions come from many sources including city or county governments, a local chamber of commerce, neighborhood associations, or state departments of transportation. Numerous resources also exist on the Internet. Google Maps, the United States Census, and the National Association of Counties can provide information on the boundaries and size of geographic communities.

Question 2 asks you to provide flavor by describing the community you plan to study in your own words. Question 3 asks you to document

Worksheet 1. Define Your Community

Question 1a	Is your community geographic, organizational, or cultural?
Question 1b	If your community is geographic, then define the boundaries of your community's location and describe its size.
Question 2	Describe your community. What is its culture like? Is it rural or urban? What kind of climate does it experience? What values, attitudes, and beliefs are most important? What kind of jobs do people have? Are there dominant religions?
Question 3	Document your community demographics including the total population, the median age, the percentage of the population in various ethnic groups, the percentage of the population with specific levels of education, and the median household income. If important to your community, you may also include the percentage of your population in each gender category, the percentage of the population that speaks specific languages, marital status, and other culturally relevant demographics.

Total population
Median age

White
Black
American Indian or Alaska Native
Asian
Native Hawaiian and other Pacific Islanders
Persons reporting two or more races

Hispanic or Latino
Not Hispanic or Latino

Non-high school graduates
High school diploma or equivalent
Some college with no degree
Associate degree
Bachelor's degree
Master's degree
Professional degree
Doctorate degree

Median household income

Question 4	In sum, what makes your community unique?

Question 5	Where did you find the information to answer the above questions?

the specific demographics of your community. You can accomplish this most easily for a geographic community by going to the U.S. Census Bureau's "American FactFinder" and searching for your city/town, county, or zip code and selecting your state (search online for http://www .census.gov). The United States Census also provides information on Tribal Statistical Areas. If you define your community as a less traditional location or as an organizational or cultural community, then you will need to become more creative in your search for demographic data. Neighborhood, religious, or professional organizations might have the data you need. The Internet may well provide some relevant statistics, but it is also worth your time to query the stakeholders in your community to find other interesting and accurate demographic information. I have provided demographic categories in question 3 that match those most often used by social service providers and are available from the United States Census. Nevertheless, you should consider your answer to question 2 and identify any other relevant demographic categories. For example, having a large population of immigrants who speak a language other than English at home may be invaluable information to know as you move forward with the needs assessment. Finally, question 4 asks you to reflect upon what you have learned about your community and summarize it in one or two sentences, and question 5 requires you to document your sources for all this information.

TASK 2: CREATE A NEEDS ASSESSMENT WORKGROUP

Once you have finished worksheet 1 and gained an appreciation of your community, you need to form a needs assessment workgroup. Altschuld and Witkin (2000) refer to this as a needs assessment committee, but I prefer the term *workgroup* because it implies that the group will do more than make decisions—they will labor. However, I do agree with their assertion, "Without the right kind of leadership and a strong, sustained commitment to the endeavor, the likelihood of the NA [needs assessment] resulting in organizational change is seriously diminished" (p. 21). You may feel comfortable leading this group or in having another member lead the group. Most importantly, the group needs an identified leader. The role of the leader is multifaceted. They must facilitate meetings and keep the group on task; they must make sure products like worksheets are completed in a timely manner; they must ensure the process is driven by data and not politics; they must become the face of the workgroup. Other members of the workgroup should either possess important data or love to work with data (preferably both). In my experience working with large and small needs assessments, it is a group made up of members who truly believe in a data-driven process that produces and later uses a quality needs assessment. Worksheet 2 asks you to identify and assemble your workgroup.

Ask yourself two questions about assembling the needs assessment workgroup. First, how big should I make my workgroup? Certainly, you can more easily manage a smaller workgroup. A larger workgroup can accomplish more in a shorter time period. My practical rule comes from the implementation of focus groups. Too few participants can lead to biased representation and a lack of real discussion. Too many participants can lead to monopolization of the work by a smaller group and a lack of engagement by other members. With this in mind, create a workgroup with roughly ten members. Worksheet 2 contains spots for a leader plus twelve potential members. Do not feel compelled to fill in each row. Let your group come together naturally with ideally between eight and twelve members.

Second, what sort of diversity should my workgroup represent? Every needs assessment workgroup will look different, but representation should reflect the providers of social services and the consumers of those services. For example, if you define your community as ninth through twelfth graders in a specific school district and are interested in the consequences of youth alcohol use, then your workgroup may include teachers, prevention coalition members, law enforcement officers, and students. Consumer groups should be included not as token members of the workgroup but as meaningful partners who are engaged in the tasks at hand. In order to ensure diversity and significant involvement, worksheet 2 includes columns describing each member's organization and the contribution they will make to the process. While initial creation of the needs assessment workgroup helps to lay the foundation for the project, membership should be continually evaluated. During the research process it may become clear that a specific sector of your community needs representation. Feel free to add that type of representation, but also keep in mind the necessary commitment of members to a data-driven process.

Worksheet 2. Assemble Your Needs Assessment Workgroup

Name	Organization	Contribution
Leader:		

After all, this is not a group charged with implementing social services; instead, it is a group devoted to data-driven decision-making regarding those services.

Remember, workgroups are rarely free-standing. Your workgroup is likely to be aligned with or part of an existing organization (for example, a mental health center, county department of health, or community coalition). Consider the sponsoring organization as you create the workgroup and its modes of operation. This along with the research questions detailed in the next section will help define the scope of the responsibility of workgroup members.

TASK 3: IDENTIFY YOUR RESEARCH QUESTIONS

The final piece of a solid foundation involves detailing your research questions. Quality scientific inquiry starts with a good question. You may create one or more questions depending upon the scope of your research and your workgroup's ambition. Worksheet 3 requires you to document your research questions. Your leader should facilitate the creation of these questions with the needs assessment workgroup. Chapter 1 discusses the difference between needs assessment research questions based upon individual services and those based upon entire communities. The latter are broader and often more complicated. In facilitating this discussion, several questions can help the workgroup narrow their concerns and interests. These queries funnel the discussion from broad to specific in order to help identify your research questions.

> What are we hoping to learn from this needs assessment?
> What social service areas should the needs assessment include?
> What populations within our defined community are we
>   specifically interested in?
> What would we most like to learn about these populations and
>   their need for social services?
> Which of the things we want to learn are of the highest priority?

Once this discussion has taken place, the needs assessment workgroup leader can begin to craft research questions with the help of workgroup members. This may occur during a meeting or between meetings. However, it is important that the workgroup agree on and buy into the research questions. Any quality research question should be open-ended (leaving room for a variety of interesting answers) but also targeted (pointing the way to action). Examples of research questions that drive a community-level needs assessment include the following: What is the biggest substance abuse-related problem among youth in our county? What service is most needed among the elderly in our tribe? Which population groups in our city are failing to receive the services we offer? What can we do to make workers in the trucking industry healthier? Worksheet 3 asks you to detail your research questions.

You may have multiple research questions, or you might only have one research question. I have included spaces for three questions on the worksheet. If you have more than three questions, then reconsider the scope of your needs assessment. Do you really have the time and resources

Worksheet 3. Detail Your Research Questions

Research Question 1

Research Question 2

Research Question 3

necessary to tackle this much research? Can you rework the questions into one or two more comprehensive questions? Take your time in writing these questions the way you might take your time in developing a new mission statement for your organization. Once they are written, put them aside for at least one day and then revisit them to ensure you are asking precisely what you wish to know.

DEMONSTRATION 1: A RURAL NEEDS ASSESSMENT WORKGROUP

In 2010, a rural Western county with an economy based on energy resources and tourism became concerned with the myriad of social problems that had arisen in their population of only 10,000 people. A caring, coordinated group of social service providers, ranging from the school superintendent to a public health coordinator, met regularly to discuss their common issues and efforts. At one of these meetings, it became clear they needed a better understanding of the problems affecting the people of their county. They decided to take on a needs assessment and started by creating a subcommittee of their larger group made up of individuals who had data to share and showed a real interest in the needs assessment process. Over the course of the yearlong project, this group evolved. It started with roughly ten members, including a researcher who facilitated the meetings and a graduate student who was responsible for working with data as prescribed by the group. Other initial members included the school superintendent, the director of a pregnancy resource center, substance abuse treatment providers, a drug court coordinator, a public health response coordinator, a provider of services for victims of sexual assault and domestic violence, and even an individual who ran the local food bank. A couple of these members failed to attend more than the first two meetings, but new members joined, including the coordinator of a local prevention coalition and an individual who worked with the elderly.

Notably, the membership of this group failed to include involvement from all of the social service providers or from the countless consumers of social services in the county. Members and the leader did not believe universal involvement was feasible considering the scope of their project; instead, they made every effort to equitably consider all potential stakeholders. This may or may not have led to bias in the group's ability to gather and consider data, but it was a logistical reality.

During its initial meeting the needs assessment workgroup completed two tasks. First, they identified potential members that should be invited to participate in the research. While they knew it was not possible to include everyone, they did identify specific stakeholders and sectors key to completing the needs assessment. This explains some of the membership evolution over time. Second, they worked to document their research questions. This proved difficult because their scope was so large. Members expressed a variety of hopes for what might be learned from the needs assessment, and all agreed the needs assessment should target the entire 10,000-person population of the county. They also agreed they lacked solid information on their biggest problems: underserved populations, and shortage of services. These concerns led them to construct the following questions: What are our biggest social problems? What subsets of our population are experiencing these problems? While neither of these research questions is groundbreaking, the example of this rural county is informative. The process of creating a workgroup provided insight into the stakeholders for the research, as well as potential challenges in completing it. The process of detailing their research questions created commitment from members to participate in the research.

The county described in demonstration 1 eventually completed their needs assessment and identified alcohol abuse, the lack of prenatal care, and poverty among single women as their largest problems. They used this information to make decisions around social service provision. Of course, moving from research questions to answers involved much toil by the group. This type of work is the subject of step 2 of this workbook. Now that you have defined your community, created a needs assessment workgroup, and detailed your research questions, you must turn to systematically gathering data. The next section leads you through the collection and analysis of data. It includes chapters on types of data, qualitative data collection and analysis, and quantitative data collection and analysis. By the end of step 2 you will have the necessary information to answer your research questions and put your needs assessment to good use.

FURTHER READINGS

To learn more about creating and facilitating a needs assessment workgroup as well as group processes, consider reading one of the following texts.

Altschuld, J. W., & Witkin, B. R. (2000). *From needs assessment to action: Transforming needs into solution strategies.* Thousand Oaks, CA: Sage Publications.

Baron, R. S., & Kerr, N. L. (2003). *Group process, group decision, group action.* Philadelphia: Open University Press.

To better understand research problems and how to ask research questions, refer to any social science research text. Two of my favorites are:

Frankfort-Nachmias, C., & Nachmias, D. (2007). *Research methods in the social sciences.* New York: Worth Publishing.

Salkind, N. J. (2012). *Exploring research.* Upper Saddle River, NJ: Pearson Education.

COLLECTING AND ANALYZING DATA

Step 2 of this workbook leads you through the collection and analysis of data. It includes chapters on types of data, qualitative data collection and analysis, and quantitative data collection and analysis. You will encounter several tasks within these chapters that help you identify and gather data for your community needs assessment. You will also find a number of useful tools and demonstrations to help build your capacity and confidence around using data. By the end of step 2, you will make generalizations and discoveries from your data that provide the necessary information to answer your research questions and make quality data-driven decisions.

THE LEARNING TAKEAWAYS FOR STEP 2 INCLUDE:

- The many types of data that can contribute to a quality needs assessment
- How to rigorously collect qualitative data
- How to rigorously collect quantitative data
- How to effectively analyze your data and draw useful conclusions from it

Types of Data

The first step in collecting data is to decide what type of data will help you and the needs assessment workgroup best answer your research questions. While training numerous groups on needs assessment and program evaluation, I have noticed a general fear of the nearly infinite amount of data that can be used or gathered for social service research. This fear also applies to the number of ways data can be collected, and it can paralyze a needs assessment workgroup or individuals trying to complete a needs assessment. "Where do we start?" might be a common and daunting question. On the other hand, workgroups often see needs assessment as synonymous with a survey. This view is shortsighted because needs assessment data can be so much more than a survey of a community or of the potential consumers of your service. I recently met with a community that wanted a needs assessment and had the necessary resources to pay for it. They immediately asked me when I could start the survey process, how large a sample they would need, and how much a survey would cost. They were surprised when I explained to them that based upon their research question they did not need a survey. Most of the necessary data already existed. What they really needed was for someone to gather together and analyze their existing archived data. This chapter outlines the finite ways data can be collected and requires you to identify which of these data collection methods you will use in completing your needs assessment.

The word *data* simply describes pieces of useful information. A needs assessment should be as scientific as possible. This means that the collection of these useful pieces of information should also be as systematic and without bias as possible. One goal of quality research is to provide accurate data, and the goal of your needs assessment is to use this accurate data to make good decisions. Your decisions are only as good as the information you use. Not only is it important to collect accurate information but also the correct information. For these reasons, you need to consider the types of data you will collect. Data is either qualitative or quantitative, and there are only a few data collection methods in each of these two categories. The following sections describe each type of data collection method to help you make an informed decision on the most useful kinds of data for your needs assessment.

QUALITATIVE DATA

Qualitative data are pieces of information in the form of words rather than numbers. Qualitative research has always been important in the social sciences and more recently in the creation of needs assessments. It can provide a deep understanding of need, an understandable analysis for stakeholders, and spice to your needs assessment. In "Qualitative Data Analysis" Miles and Huberman (1994) claim, "Qualitative data are sexy. They are a source of well-grounded, rich descriptions and explanations of processes in identifiable local contexts" (p. 1). Sexy does not imply simple, however. Qualitative research is based upon a number of methodological traditions. These include phenomenology (focusing on the subjective experience of the individual), grounded theory (creating an explanation of experience based upon interviews and observations), ethnography (describing and interpreting group culture), and more (Merriam, 2002). Most important for your needs assessment is understanding that in qualitative research you are the instrument that amasses the data. Qualitative data can provide meaning and context to your needs assessment, and they are gathered in one of four ways.

Interviews

Often, change on any issue is only possible when the community is ready to make this change. Community readiness is an important factor across social service areas, and I have seen it measured as part of needs assessments for sexual violence, HIV/AIDS, substance abuse, and public health. In each of these cases, the standard assessment of community readiness comes from interviews with key community stakeholders. For a project in Oregon, we wanted to understand how prepared the state was to prevent high-risk alcohol use among young adults. This involved the adaptation of an accepted instrument to measure readiness (Plested, Edwards, & Jumper-Thurman, 2006) and interviews with twenty-five individuals from various sectors. Combining and analyzing the results of these interviews provided a deeper understanding of the state's need, as well as a definite level of readiness. We used the data to recommend specific actions to build the capacity and increase the readiness to do something about high-risk drinking among young adults. None of this would have been possible without interviewing key stakeholders, and interviews like this might be very useful in your needs assessment as well.

In general, qualitative research can provide a deeper understanding of issues and processes than its quantitative counterpart. The purpose of the qualitative interview is to probe individuals for this deeper meaning. For example, a quantitative survey may ask for a respondent's feelings on a five-point scale, but a qualitative interview allows the respondent to describe and explain those feelings. This makes a qualitative interview very different than a quantitative survey. You will have only a handful of interviewees; you will hand-pick these interviewees; you will engage the interviewees in discussion. According to Taylor and Bogdan (1998), "qualitative interviewing is flexible and dynamic" (p. 88). This all means that interviews may be the correct data collection method for your needs assessment if a small number of key stakeholders have in-depth knowledge of the issue you are studying and can help to answer your identified research questions. In the Oregon example above, we realized that only the key stakeholders within and around state government could truly describe for us the capacity and readiness of the system in which they worked.

Often interviews are described as structured, semi-structured, or unstructured. I like to think of interviews as ranging between highly structured interchanges to open-ended unstructured discussions. In reality, if you choose to implement interviews as part of your needs assessment, you will do a little of everything. If you are interviewing the local chief of police about vandalism in a downtown entertainment district, then structured questions may include the following.

> How many acts of vandalism occur each weekend in the
> downtown?
> How many arrests has your department made downtown in the
> past year?
> What time of day does downtown vandalism usually occur?

You will also want to include less structured questions that probe the police chief's knowledge of the situation.

> What have downtown business owners been doing to address
> vandalism?
> How has the problem of downtown vandalism changed over time?
> Who do you think is mostly responsible for the vandalism?

Finally, you will want to engage the police chief in a deeper discussion of the issue with very open-ended questions.

> Can you describe specific incidences of vandalism you have seen?
> What do you believe are the factors causing downtown vandalism?
> What solutions to vandalism would you like to see implemented
> downtown?

As the interview moves from structured to open-ended questions, the interviewer will also ask follow-up questions to help the police chief better articulate his answers.

Other important aspects of qualitative interviewing include selecting the informants, becoming a good interviewer, and documenting the conversation. The latter is most often done by recording the interview and taking notes at the same time. Ideally, two researchers show up to conduct an interview. The first is responsible for asking the questions and engaging the informant in discussion. The second is responsible for audio recording and taking notes. However, ideal is not always realistic. I have conducted interviews alone, without audio recording equipment, and even over the telephone. Interviews might also be conducted over the Internet.

There are always tradeoffs when conducting interviews, but you should strive to be the best interviewer possible. If that is not your skill set, then choose a different member of the needs assessment workgroup to implement the interviews. The most important trait of a good interviewer is being a good listener, but other aspects of interviewing are also very important. A talented interviewer is nonjudgmental, sensitive, and a good conversationalist. Interviews go very well when the interviewer gets the informant to talk about what is important to them (Taylor & Bogdan, 1998). Lastly, qualitative data collected through interviews is only as good as your selection of informants. There is no right or wrong number of people to interview. Resources, proximity, and time all play a role in choosing who and how many people to interview. Kvale (1996) points out that you should "interview as many subjects as necessary to find out what you need to know" (p. 101).

Choosing qualitative interviews as a data collection method in your needs assessment is dependent upon your research questions. These questions will also help you decide who and how many informants to interview. In general, select to interview key stakeholders if your research questions require in-depth knowledge held by a small number of individuals.

Focus Groups

Focus groups are interviews held with a group of individuals rather than a single individual. Their power lies in a depth of discussion that only a group can bring out. Consider how different conversation is when you have coffee with one friend compared to a dinner party with many friends. The same is true when it comes to interviewing an individual compared to a group. With an interview, you want to learn about an individual's experiences and knowledge; with a focus group you want to learn about the group's experiences and knowledge. As part of recent research on suicide prevention, I had the opportunity to conduct focus groups with specific sets of college students. This included resident assistants who supervised younger students in dormitories, students from other countries, and student members of the Reserve Officers' Training Corps (ROTC). Our goal was to learn more about how to better prevent suicide on college campuses among at-risk populations. With American soldiers returning from war in Iraq and Afghanistan, the final group was particularly fascinating. It took a while for the group discussion to move beyond niceties and clichés, but when it did, the ROTC members as a group truly enlightened us in ways that individuals could not have. Nor could a survey of soldiers have provided us with the kind of stories or emotions that these young people offered. In the end, our campus media and outreach campaign was dramatically altered because of a ninety-minute discussion with eight very honest students.

Notice from this example, focus groups target specific collections of individuals (usually between 8 and 12) who have a common experience or knowledge of an issue. I am constantly amazed by communities who have used focus groups for needs assessments and make two huge mistakes. First, they try to gather a random sample of participants. This, they believe, creates more generalizable results, but the point of a focus group is not to generalize findings to a whole population. Focus groups provide a depth of understanding for specific populations. Second, they create descriptive statistics from the answers the group provides. For example, 30 percent of focus group participants said they believed homelessness was the biggest problem in our community, 60 percent believed underage drinking is the biggest problem in our community, and the other 10 percent believed spousal abuse is the biggest problem in our community. If generalizable descriptive statistics is what you need, then maybe a telephone survey is the data collection methodology you should use. Krueger (1994) articulates this when he writes the purpose of focus groups "is to obtain information of a qualitative nature from a predetermined and limited number of people" (pp. 14–15).

Like conducting an interview, facilitating a focus group takes practice and skill. Most important are the abilities to actively listen and lead a discussion. If you choose to use focus groups as part of your needs assessment, then you should also choose wisely among members of your needs assessment workgroup to facilitate the effort. My wife often reminds me I am a better talker than listener. This means I usually either choose someone else to run focus groups as part of my research or work terrifically hard during group facilitation. But do not let facilitating a focus group scare you off. In the end, you simply have to ask open-ended questions that lead to discussion and provide a safe environment where participants can share their experiences and feelings. The facilitator must also manage the group process—making sure only one person talks at a time, keeping single individuals from monopolizing the discussion, or bringing quiet individuals into the conversation.

Of course, group membership and location of the focus group also play a role and both need to be chosen carefully. Typically more than one focus group is necessary. Do you have the same targeted subjects in each? Do you have one with men and one with women? Do you recruit participants based upon demographics like age and race? Or do you run three or four focus groups with the same populations and look for similarities? All of these questions are best answered by looking back at your needs assessment research questions. Location is important because you want participants to feel safe and at ease. You also want to burden them as little as possible. It is difficult enough to find participants without making them drive an hour to the focus group or starting at ten o'clock in the evening. Early in my career the location of a focus group provided detail into the problem I was researching. I was interested in the causes of underage drinking in rural Nebraska and conducted a number of focus groups with teenagers in small towns. Local adults arranged for teens to show up, pizzas to be delivered, and for a quiet place where we could have the conversation. Directions to the first focus group included the phrase "turn left immediately after the super liquor market." The somewhat private back room of the small pizza restaurant where I facilitated the focus group was mostly lit by neon advertisements for beer. During the conversation the young participants expressed how strong the drinking culture was in their community and how hard it was for a young person to not grow up drinking alcohol when you live in this culture. The location chosen by adults seemed to provide evidence of this as well.

Similar to interviews, focus groups use a range of structured, semi-structured, and unstructured questions. The order and use of these questions is more important in a group discussion than in an individual interview, and focus groups will contain many more open-ended questions than an interview likely will. The questions need to slowly help participants open up while narrowing the conversation toward your targeted concerns. These questions would obviously reflect the research questions driving your needs assessment. Early in the focus group you may ask each participant to answer a simple and nonthreatening question to make them feel comfortable with talking in front of others. The following question might play that role using the example of downtown vandalism.

What did you do the last time you visited the downtown?

Later questions dig deeper, trying to elicit group discussion while still reflecting the overall research question of the needs assessment.

What factors do you believe are causing vandalism in our downtown?

A good facilitator will continue to probe the group for answers and try to have members respond to each other. Note that this question is nearly identical to a question asked in an interview of the police chief, but also understand that group discussion will lead to very different answers than simply asking the chief of police. The real power of a focus group is in what happens when participants react to each other, and you will initially look for consensus or disagreement among the group.

Choosing to implement focus groups as part of your needs assessment should be based upon your research questions. If you are trying to gain a deeper understanding of an issue, if you need to discover differences between sets of people, or if you simply need to learn more about the experiences and knowledge of a targeted population, then focus groups might be the best way to collect data.

Observations

Observation is the basis of all research and can lead to data collection in the form of words as well as numbers. Think of all that has been learned by primatologist Jane Goodall, who lived among, observed, and wrote about chimpanzees and gorillas. We learned that primates use tools, have a darker side, and even fight wars. Similarly, you can use observation in your needs assessment to learn things about your community that will help to answer your research questions. I once worked with a college public health class to complete an environmental scan. The project served as both a learning experience for the students and as important information for the campus prevention coalition. We sent students out in pairs to observe the campus environment. The observations were structured and included categories like campus life, alcohol availability and promotion, media, campus bookstore, and student neighborhoods. We encouraged the students to approach the campus from any direction and to attend events they were interested in. We armed them with paper and pencil for writing their observations as well as disposable cameras for capturing particularly interesting images. The structure provided some opportunity for quantitative data collection. For example, 21.4 percent of our student teams observed beer pyramids in apartment windows in the student neighborhoods. But, more importantly, the students documented their observations in words. "We noticed that all bars have the university logo," "Alcohol seems to be promoted everywhere you look," and "Alcohol is readily available on campus and advertisements for parties and bars were on bulletin boards" were the kind of statements that really helped the coalition understand the causes of alcohol misuse on campus. In partic- ular, students observed alcohol was scarce and rarely advertised at sport- ing events, but the campus bookstore was full of messages promoting overconsumption and sold shot glasses and beer mugs despite many stu- dents being underage.

If you choose observation as a qualitative data collection method in your needs assessment, then several decisions must be made. First, con- sider whether the observation will be passive or participatory. Passive observation is likely what you initially considered at the start of this sec- tion. If you want to know about behavior differences among male and female teenagers at a dance, then you would sit in a chair and watch them interact. If you want to know how runners feel at different stages of a marathon, then you might watch them start, drive to mile 15 and watch them pass, and drive to mile 26 and watch them finish. However, those are passive observations. You may want to do more than watch others run a marathon; you may want to run it yourself and report on what you saw, smelled, heard, and felt while participating in the race. Neither role is preferable, and you can choose a path somewhere between passive and participatory observation. Creswell (2007) especially appreciates an evolv- ing role where the observer begins as an outsider and becomes an insider over time. The decision on the role of the observer should be made based upon the needs assessment research questions.

Second, you must decide when and where to observe. Qualitative observation is necessarily fieldwork, so your choice of fields is important. For example, you may want to understand shopping patterns and behav- iors during the holiday season. Does this mean observing shoppers in large discount stores like Target or Walmart, or do you observe shoppers in small independent shops in your quaint downtown? Does this mean observing shoppers at night, on the weekend, during early morning "Black Friday" sales, on one day, or over several weeks? Do you do all of these things or just a few?

Third, you need to decide what exactly to observe. Observation can quickly become vast and overwhelming. In the above example of a campus environmental scan, student observers were given very prescriptive protocols to keep the scope of the research within reason. If we had given them blank pages with the directive "write down everything you see that has to do with alcohol on campus," then they would have reported back an endless variety of observations. Similarly, if you go to observe holiday shoppers in large discount stores, then you would want to provide structure in the form of open-ended questions like the following.

Describe the attitudes that holiday shoppers have while they are moving around the store.

How do holiday shoppers seem to make decisions about purchases?

What differences in behavior are there between holiday shoppers of different ages and genders?

Again, answers to queries about where, when, and what to observe are driven by your research questions and, of course, your available resources. Once you understand the role of the observer and know where, when, and what you are observing, you will create a protocol to give your qualitative observation structure.

Choosing qualitative observation as a data collection method in your needs assessment is dependent upon your research questions. These questions will also help you define the scope of your observations and the field research you intend to complete. In general, select qualitative observation if you want data that comes from the arena you consider your community and is not filtered through another mechanism like a survey or the opinions of key stakeholders. Observational data are directly seen, heard, or felt by you or your needs assessment workgroup.

Archives

When embarking upon a needs assessment of any kind, people often assume they must conduct original research. However, abundant qualitative information may already exist. Data that already exists can be found in archives, and you may discover archival data very illuminating. These are often called source documents or secondary data because they don't require primary research like focus groups or observations. My favorite story about archival information took place at the American Heritage Center (AHC) at the University of Wyoming. This center serves as the repository for manuscript collections, rare books, and a number of university archives. Scholars from around the world come to the AHC to study and look through the mostly qualitative and historical archival materials. One important collection includes the works of Owen Wister, a frequent visitor to the American West and Wyoming. Wister's most famous novel was the story of a cowboy caught up in the Johnson County War titled *The Virginian: A Horseman of the Plains*. The book is regarded as the first cowboy western novel and was dedicated to Wister's friend Theodore Roosevelt. It seems only natural that Wister's collection resides at the University of Wyoming. This collection includes his large writing desk, which had been on display for years. As a student, I volunteered at the AHC during its move to a wonderful new building. When several young men came to move Wister's incredibly heavy desk, the first thing they did was take out all the drawers in order to lighten the load. The desk had been on display so long that no one had ever thought to open the drawers. Inside were a number of Owen Wister's journals that scholars had never before seen. These journals represented an amazing new set of qualitative archival data.

Old journals likely will not help you with a social service needs assessment, but I hope you understand that mountains of relevant information that can help answer your research questions already exist. This data may be found in libraries or public archives like the AHC mentioned above, on a seemingly endless list of Internet web pages, or most often as part of organizational record keeping. Let us take each of these in turn. Libraries and archives will most likely provide historical data on your community. Many times a needs assessment requires background information as to whether your community is geographic, organizational, or cultural. For example, a local bilingual radio station in my home town is a not-for-profit organization that plays mostly Spanish-language programs. While they serve the entire geographic community, their target audience includes a small but important Hispanic population. When writing grants, developing programming, or reaching out to their community, they need to understand the people they serve. This might mean conducting key interviews with stakeholders or focus groups with listeners, but it also means knowing why and how the Hispanic population came to live in this community. Archives at the public library can provide this information. Stories of Hispanic railroad workers who helped settle the town or families who played a role in developing its infrastructure provide real context to any needs assessment the radio station might create.

However, libraries and archives do a poor job of providing the most recent qualitative archival data. The Internet can provide data that is only moments old, and it may be useful in understanding needs. For example, many discussion forums exist for the public to ask and answer questions on an endless array of topics. I recently logged on to the Stop Abuse for Everyone (SAFE) website (http://www.safe4all.org). SAFE is an organization that provides services to victims of domestic violence who often fall between the cracks. This includes straight and gay men, teens, and the elderly. Their support and discussion forum is full of tragic stories of cruelty and abuse. One man posted a story of feeling low and useless and the constant criticism from his partner. Others wrote about trying to save their brother or mother, about how their sad story came to a hopeful end, and about becoming more and more isolated. The forum provides an outlet for individuals in need as well as advice from others who have experienced similar difficulties, but viewed from a different perspective the forum also provides a rich source of qualitative data. These stories give context to SAFE's work, and their analysis can certainly inform any needs assessment undertaken by the SAFE organization.

Finally, piles of information exist as organizational records. A professor in graduate school once told me "files are the life blood of any bureaucracy." Every business, government, or not-for-profit organization keeps records of their work. Indeed even the smallest organizations have qualitative archives. During the long Wyoming winters, I coach short-track ice speed skating at our local ice arena. We coaches volunteer our time; we have no budget; we derive our energy from the enthusiasm of the youth participants; and we have qualitative archives. We used photos of the kids racing, a scrapbook of our early years, and lists of race participants to successfully complete the needs assessment section of a grant for new skates. Similarly, your organization will possess records of past and current goals, activities, and accomplishments. Thinking about the above example of downtown vandalism, you may be able to access police records of reported crimes, insurance claims for property damage, or the bookkeeping of downtown businesses (of course, these can provide quantitative data as well). If your assessment involves the need for healthy eating alternatives, then you may be able to collect local restaurant menus. Or if your assessment involves workforce development in a specific field in your community, then you may be able to find and use files of past job applicants. Possible sources for organizational records are only limited by the vast amount of records kept in today's world.

While archives provide an easily accessible source of data that often requires few resources, their vastness can become overwhelming. Limit the qualitative archives used as a data collection method in your needs assessment by focusing upon your research questions. In general, select qualitative archives if you need historical information, information on organizations, or information that is readily available and does not require original research.

QUANTITATIVE DATA

Quantitative data are pieces of information in the form of numbers rather than words. Quantitative research will provide the backbone and structure to any needs assessment. While your needs assessment may or may not find qualitative data useful, research using numbers is most likely a necessary part of the needs assessment. Quantitative data provide the hard-and-fast facts and an often easily understood way of determining need. Organizations of all sizes and types rely upon quantitative measures to better understand their need, scope, and progress. Welch and Comer (2006) write, "Clearly, familiarity with statistics is necessary to survive and be successful in bureaucracies" (p. 3). Please do not let the word *statistics* frighten you away from continuing with your needs assessment. Statistics are really just a way to simplify, organize, and manipulate data to answer your research questions (Healey, 2012). They can be either descriptive (summarizing the data about the group being studied) or inferential (making generalizations from a sample to the larger population of interest). Quantitative data can provide meaning to your needs assessment through simple and convincing numbers, and they are gathered in one of three ways.

Surveys

Surveys are a type of research instrument that asks people a series of questions, and you would be hard pressed to find an American (young or old) who has not responded to at least one survey in their lifetime. Surveys have become so ubiquitous in America that scarcely a day can go by without seeing or reading the results. Many of these results come from opinion polls and provide information on our approval or disapproval of American presidents, our like or dislike of particular television shows, or our concerns and beliefs surrounding policy issues. Johnson, Joslyn, and Reynolds (2001) remark, "as the use of surveys as a research method has grown, so too has the amount of research on the method itself" (p. 276). In other words, the survey research field has become incredibly sophisticated in its methodology and its ability to answer questions about public opinion, perception, and need. This final aspect may be really useful in your needs assessment work.

Surveys can be completed in any number of ways. Most people think first of telephone surveyors who interrupt their dinner to ask a series of questions about a range of topics. My department houses the University of Wyoming Survey Research Center. Late in the afternoon, I often overhear student workers sitting in front of a computer in cubicles and wearing headsets asking a respondent on the other end of the line how many times in the past month they have smoked at least one cigarette or which candidate they would vote for if the election were held today. But surveys can also be done on the Internet, through the mail, or in person. I have worked with people who have "intercepted" individuals in shopping malls and on hiking trails in national parks. I have seen surveys on the tables in restaurants and on store receipts. Some surveys include captive audiences in classrooms while others rely upon a convenient population of volunteers who want to voice their opinions. The point is, we have grown to see real value in finding out what people believe and how they behave by simply asking them. This means that a survey may provide you with worthwhile information about the needs of your community.

A colleague of mine is the principal investigator of a survey called the Wyoming Prevention Needs Assessment. It is a paper and pencil survey administered to all sixth-, eighth-, tenth-, and twelfth-grade students throughout the state. He biannually receives nearly 20,000 completed surveys. These answers are scanned by computer, cleaned by staff, and analyzed through automation. The results provide state-level quantitative information on substance use among youth as well as a host of risk and protective factors. He provides the same information for each county and school district in Wyoming. As a needs assessment the information is incredibly valuable. The state, schools, and communities use this needs assessment survey to plan programming and policy change. They trend data to evaluate efforts, and they use the information to make funding decisions. In short, the Prevention Needs Assessment in Wyoming provides much of the information communities use to answer their prevention research questions.

However, surveys need not be this large or involved to provide interesting and valuable information. I once helped my own community survey liquor license holders to determine their need for education around the license renewal process and alcohol server training options. Results showed that license holders preferred regular police checks, failure of an underage drinking compliance check, and violations that lead to convictions be used as criteria for license renewal. Also, 71 percent of the respondents wanted the city to require on-site responsible beverage service training for their managers and other staff. Responses to the one-page survey from only twenty-five license holders helped the city council reshape their policies based upon the needs and opinions of local business owners.

Large and small surveys, like the two mentioned above, have a number of things in common. First, they are made up of high-quality questions that lead to quantitative information. In the above qualitative discussion, I provide examples of open-ended questions used in interviews or focus groups. For instance, how has the problem of downtown vandalism changed over time? This may lead to important data. But questions on a quantitative survey must lead to numbered values. This type of question is asked with or without answer choices provided. Consider a quick and simple example.

Are you male? _____ or female? _____

This question provides answer choices, but it could also be asked without providing these choices.

What is your gender? _____

And, yes, this is a quantitative question because the answer choices can be scored as male equals 1 and female equals 2. I discuss analyzing data like this in chapter 7, but I hope you see it is the counts of 1's and 2's that might allow you to claim that 32 percent of survey respondents are male and 68 percent are female. Similarly, we can ask respondents about their age with or without answer choices.

How old are you? _____
Which of the following age categories best describes you?
_____ 35 or younger
_____ 36 to 65
_____ 66 or older

Again, answers provide numbers—in the first, an actual age like 27 or 53, and in the second, an age category score of 1, 2, or 3. By having this type of data, you may be able to provide information about the average or typical age group of your respondents. More interesting, however, are quantitative measures of beliefs, attitudes, and behaviors. These most often come with answer choices in the form of scales. For example,

How safe is the community where you live?
_____ very unsafe
_____ somewhat unsafe
_____ somewhat safe
_____ very safe

This type of question provides counts when scored 1 (very unsafe), 2 (somewhat unsafe), 3 (somewhat safe), and 4 (very safe) as well as a ranking of these scores. The gender question above just gives us categories, but here we can actually interpret a score of 3 as a greater feeling of safety than a score of 1. Someone with a score of 2 feels more unsafe than someone with a score of 4. Now consider the potential of asking gender, age, and a question about safety on your needs assessment survey. We would be able to answer questions like: do men or women feel less safe in our community? Or what age group of people in our community feels the safest?

Choosing to conduct a survey as part of your needs assessment should be based upon your research questions, and while surveys are a common needs assessment tool, they are not required. Many high-quality and useful needs assessments are completed without survey research. However, if you want to better understand the attitudes, beliefs, and behaviors of your entire community or of a target population within your community, then a survey can be an incredibly useful way to collect quantitative data. Select a survey to help answer your research questions when aggregating individual answers to questions helps paint a picture of community needs.

Observations

Again, observation is the basis of all science. In a quantitative context, this simply means counting things that happen. As a teenager, several friends and I were paid a small sum to sit in the parking lot of a new strip mall and count the number of cars traveling by in either direction. We worked in four-hour shifts to collect the accurate (though this is a strong word to apply to the work of teenagers at two o'clock in the morning) number of cars that drove by at different times of the day. My memory is eating corn chips and drinking soda while hoping a car might drive by, but I assume the data was used by strip mall developers to market and understand potential crowds. In graduate school, I actually met a young woman whose father invented the black cables that stretch across streets and highways to measure traffic flow. While the black cable is undoubtedly more accurate and requires fewer corn chips than teenage boys, both represent instruments to gather quantitative observations. Often communities fail to realize they have the potential to understand need by simply counting things.

Revisiting the example of downtown vandalism, we might establish need and answer research questions by strolling through the downtown and counting visible acts of vandalism, the number of people frequenting shops and restaurants, or groups of young people just "hanging out." Similarly, a community with long, cold winters wanting to understand the need for a public ice skating rink may count the number of houses in town with flooded, frozen back yards or the number of kids trying to skate on frozen ponds. Both cases highlight the advantage of quantitative observation—what Frankfort-Nachmias and Nachmias (2007) call directness. This means, instead of you as a researcher asking people for their opinions or about their behavior, you directly watch them do things. This becomes firsthand data without the filter of your subject's observations and allows you to study your community and the people in it without changing the natural environment. Think of biologists who study frogs. They often must decide between the rigor of a laboratory experiment with dozens of frogs in tanks and the natural setting of studying what frogs they can find in a pond. Both situations have value and both can be used successfully depending upon the research question, but quantitative observation as part of your community needs assessment almost always means surveillance in your community's natural setting.

The previous discussion of qualitative observation made a distinction between passive and participatory observation. In the quantitative context it is much more likely you will act as a passive observer. For example, accurately counting the number of people who walk into a building is much easier if you are not one of them. Note that, like qualitative observation, quantitative observation is research. This means you need to enter the field with, at the very least, a structured set of questions to answer but more likely a scoring or check sheet. If you want to observe the differences in drinking behavior between men and women in local taverns, then you would not simply show up with a blank journal. Instead, you would have a spreadsheet or graph paper with columns for men and women and spaces to place check marks each time a man or woman orders a drink. If you want to observe the number of new acts of downtown vandalism each week, then you would have a logbook with spaces for describing the vandalism, recording the location, and noting the date.

Chapter 5 on quantitative data collection provides more detail into how to record observations and turn them into numbers for analysis. Similar to survey results discussed above, observations leading to numbers possess tremendous potential for concretely determining need based upon empirical evidence. Select quantitative observation if you want data that comes from your community environment without being filtered through another instrument like a survey. Quantitative observation tends to require fewer resources and can supplement other data with local context based upon simple facts.

Archives

Finally, more abundant and potentially more useful than any other type of data you may use in your community needs assessment is archived quantitative data. I have completed numerous local and state-level needs assessments using only archived quantitative data. Identifying data gaps in a community can be one of your most important research questions. It is perfectly acceptable in a community needs assessment to prioritize the need for more data, and the only way to know that is to inventory the data you already have. One of my projects with the nine Tribes of Oregon began with a comprehensive needs assessment. A number of tribes immediately began planning for a survey of tribal members, but we held them back and asked them to first complete their needs assessment using existing data. The logic for this was that we could never know what questions to ask on a survey if we didn't know the current state of their data. Tribes tend to be data rich. From their schools and law enforcement to Indian Health Service agencies, most tribes and reservations I have worked with have abundant data. However, this data is rarely comprehensively organized and inventoried. Many other communities and local organizations can make the same claim. For this reason, and if your research questions lead to this, you may find archived data a valuable addition to your needs assessment.

Quantitative archived data fall into two categories. The first category is data that represents original research done by others. For example, students in schools across America are surveyed regularly about their attitudes, beliefs, and behaviors. If you want to know percentages of teens that wear seat belts, smoke cigarettes, or have been forced to have intercourse against their will, then the Youth Risk Behavior Survey is the place to look. If you want to know about college students who feel depressed or party too much, then the National College Health Assessment is your source. Similar to schools, government agencies across the country gather mountains of data. If you want to know how many arrests your local law enforcement made for violent crimes or drug crimes, then the Uniform Crime Reports are a great source. If you want to know about local unemployment rates, then look in the annual reports of your state employment agency. And, of course, the United States Census provides an endless amount of quantitative information on communities. In the preface, I mentioned a statewide comprehensive needs assessment I helped complete with Wyoming's State Epidemiological Workgroup. We looked at 269 indicators from more than 80 data sources to identify a target for the statewide prevention project. Every one of these sources fell into the category of research completed by someone else. We did not even consider original research because we knew others had done that work for us.

The second category is data that exists but no one bothered to collect, count, or summarize in meaningful ways. These types of quantitative archives are everywhere. Classroom attendance sheets, an organization's financial accounts, and library records of borrowed books are all examples of archived data waiting to help you with your needs assessment. No one has bothered to analyze these records in meaningful ways, mostly because they have not considered your research questions. While completing my dissertation on morality policies made toward the entertainment industry, I needed a quantitative measure of attention paid to moral issues in Hollywood by the press. I retreated to the university library and volumes of the *Readers' Guide to Periodical Literature* from 1902 to 1997. Today, electronic searches of this guide are commonplace, but not from as early as 1902. I wanted a consistent measure of how many articles were written each year since 1902 on the morality of entertainment. The answer sat on a shelf before me in hundreds of thousand-page volumes. No one had ever answered this question before. So I opened the *Readers' Guide* from 1902, looked up key words, and began tabulating the number of articles for each year. Several weeks later I had a quantitative measure of media attention paid to Hollywood morality for each year.

Your needs assessment will likely not involve this kind of devotion or eye strain, but remember that quantitative information is everywhere. And with the Internet, much of it comes straight to your computer. Your research questions will help you decide to look for quantitative archived data. In general, choose to use this type of data if you need an overall understanding of the community, if you plan to compare and prioritize separate problems, or if you feel like some of the data you need already exists.

TRIANGULATION

Each of the types of data discussed above has certain advantages as well as limitations. To create the best possible community needs assessment, you need to collect data in more than one way. This minimizes the limitations of each type of data while increasing your understanding of need and more accurately measuring that need. Social scientists call the process of using multiple types of data or multiple measures to answer your research question "triangulation" (Frankfort-Nachmias & Nachmias, 2007; Leary 2008). Triangulation may allow you to feel more confident in your research because you have consistent findings from different angles, or it may point out inconsistencies in your results. For example, interviews with key informants could indicate your downtown is being vandalized by loitering youth, but observation may show that youth rarely frequent the downtown, choosing to hang out at the mall instead. On the other hand, a needs assessment concerned with the causes of underage drinking might find that youth obtain most of their alcohol from parents or other adults. In my own work, I have found this to be true on student surveys, in focus groups with teens, and during interviews with law enforcement.

DEMONSTRATION 2: UNDERSTANDING SUICIDE ON A COLLEGE CAMPUS

Suicide is a difficult problem to understand in any community. College students who live off campus or go home to different states compound this difficulty. Moreover, suicides are rare and often unreported or reported as accidental deaths. So how does a college campus understand their need for suicide prevention efforts or interventions for students at risk for suicide? A state university was interested in just this question and decided to look beyond the small number of suicide deaths for which they had a record. They used several measures other than suicide deaths as surrogates or alternate variables to create a comprehensive picture of potential suicide. This variety of data provided the necessary information to plan suicide prevention efforts and make a difference on their campus.

Researchers first turned to the National College Health Assessment. This survey, done as a random sample of students in classes across campus, provided quantitative measures of everything from sexual behavior and alcohol use to depression and attempted suicide. They learned that 10 percent of students reported "seriously considering suicide" and 1 percent reported "attempting suicide." They also found that more than 70 percent of students felt "overwhelmed" by all they had to do, and nearly half binge drink at least once every two weeks. All of these measures were higher than the national average, showing that many students on campus were at risk for depression or suicidal feelings.

The university next turned to data from their own counseling center where students seeking help report the reasons for their visit on intake forms. These quantitative archives showed that 53 percent of clients came in for depression and 4 percent came in because of suicidal feelings. Finally, they interviewed key informants and students who worked as resident assistants in the campus dormitories to learn more about the culture and how to recognize at-risk students. This qualitative information helped to identify possible strategies for suicide prevention interventions.

This multimethod approach to needs assessment allowed the college to successfully seek federal campus suicide prevention funding as well as to create a comprehensive approach to suicide prevention. They created a campus coalition, implemented a media and outreach campaign, and educated faculty, staff, and students on how to recognize the signs of depression and refer students for help. After a few years of work, they saw an increase in referrals to the counseling center and students reporting seriously considering suicide decreased from 10 percent to 6 percent.

TASK 4: CHOOSE YOUR DATA COLLECTION METHODS

This chapter describes seven different ways to collect qualitative and quantitative data to answer your research questions. Your fourth task is to choose which of these methods will best help you complete the needs assessment. In choosing data collection methods, always keep your research questions in mind and consider the members of your workgroup and the skills they bring to this research. Worksheet 4 asks you to choose the types of data you will collect to best answer your research questions.

At this point, do not worry about specific measures or instruments for collecting data; rather, think about what types of data will be ideal for answering your specific needs assessment questions, and consider how

Worksheet 4. Choose Your Data Collection Methods

	Types of Data Collection and Reasons to Use Each	Will you use this data collection method in your community needs assessment?
Qualitative	Interviews: Select to interview key stakeholders if your research questions require in-depth knowledge held by a small number of individuals.	Yes _____ No _____
	Focus Groups: Select to conduct focus groups if you are trying to gain a deeper understanding of an issue or if you need to learn more about the experiences and knowledge of a targeted population.	Yes _____ No _____
	Observations: Select qualitative observation if you want data that comes from your community and is not filtered through another mechanism, like a survey or the opinions of key stakeholders.	Yes _____ No _____
	Archives: Select qualitative archives if you need historical information, information on organizations, or information that is readily available and doesn't require original research.	Yes _____ No _____
Quantitative	Survey: Select a survey to help answer your research questions when aggregating individual answers to questions into numbers helps paint a picture of community needs.	Yes _____ No _____
	Observations: Select quantitative observation when counts of people, behaviors, or objects in your community can provide context and facts to your needs assessment.	Yes _____ No _____
	Archives: Select quantitative archives if you need an overall understanding of the community, if you plan to compare and prioritize separate problems, or if you feel like some of the data you need already exists.	Yes _____ No _____

the types of data you choose to collect might work together to triangulate on your research questions. If you want to better understand the need for counseling services in your community, then you may talk to counselors and therapists (key informant interviews), consult with the State Department of Health on the number of clients and amount of funding spent locally (quantitative archives), and develop a questionnaire to be voluntarily completed by clients at public and private counseling centers (survey). Similarly, if you want to better understand the need for pedestrian walkways in a downtown area, then you might spend several days observing pedestrian walking patterns (quantitative observations) and have group discussions with downtown business owners and shoppers (focus groups).

HUMAN SUBJECT RESEARCH

Often, communities I work with have misperceptions and fears around the idea of an Institutional Review Board (the dreaded IRB). One state agency actually asked that I eliminate a deliverable in a contract stating I would seek IRB approval because they were afraid it would get in the way of the research and delay the project. While working with an IRB can take time, there is nothing to fear. Seeking IRB approval is not the same as defending a thesis or dissertation. IRBs exist in organizations like universities or state departments of health to ensure the protection of the subjects of our research. They do not tell you whether or not your research is of high quality; instead, they exist to make sure your research is ethical and does not harm the people you are studying or ultimately trying to help. In general, social service providers never use an IRB because they do not usually have access to one and their research will never be published.

My research is always subject to IRB approval, because, as a faculty member of a major university, I have access to an IRB and may publish my findings in academic journals. The distinction around publication is important. As you begin to collect data in chapters 4 and 5, you must consider whether your needs assessment is being done as "research" or "quality improvement." In other words, are you trying to add to the knowledge base of your field through academic publication or are you trying to improve social service provision in your community? In almost every case, for people working through this book, the latter is true. If you do have access to an IRB, then I suggest you use it. If you do not have access, then it probably is not necessary that you seek out an IRB and get approval. However, you should still be aware of the protection of human subjects. Even without the benefit of an IRB, you should complete ethical research that is mindful of potential risks to its subjects. The next couple of pages provide information on how to do just this.

Human subject research refers to any research where the researcher interacts with the individuals being studied. For example, you may take blood samples from new mothers or conduct a focus group with members of a high school chorus. Both have you directly collecting data from research subjects. On the other hand, you may count the number of cars in a shopping mall parking lot or find youth survey results on the Internet. These do not involve you actually interacting with human subjects to collect data. Cars in a parking lot are not human and presumably the researchers who implemented the youth survey you found on the Internet already have IRB approval for their research. This means only three of the data collection methods discussed in this chapter involve direct human subject research: focus groups, interviews, and surveys.

If you chose any of these as data collection methods, then keep a number of things in mind. First, the benefits of your research should out-weigh the risks. In general, the risks for a focus group with food cooperative users or a survey of parents are not as risky as testing new pharmaceuticals or psychological therapies, but there is still some risk. Participants may be embarrassed by the discussion or simply waste an evening of their life. You should consider the risks to your research subjects prior to collecting data.

Second, some populations are more vulnerable than others. In particular, you should be extra careful when the subjects of your research are prisoners or children. Past unethical studies of prisoners have led to strict regulations around using prisoners for research, and I would avoid this unless your needs assessment is being done in collaboration with penal institutions. In this case, they will usually have access to IRBs containing a prisoner representative to ensure human subject protection. As minors, children are unable to provide consent for participation in your needs assessment. This does not mean you cannot collect data from children. It means you must have the approval of their parents or guardians before doing so. Tool 1 is a basic template for parental consent. Adapt and use this if you plan to interview, focus group, or survey children.

Tool 1. Sample Parental Consent Form

Dear Parent(s)/Guardian(s):

Your child has an opportunity to take part in a needs assessment study being done by [describe your organization]. This [survey, focus group, or interview] collects information about [paraphrase research question]. Participation will take about [approximate time commitment] and involves [describe the process]. The purpose of this study is [describe the purpose]. The risk to your child will be [describe potential risks and benefits]. Information collected from your child will be confidential, and your child's name will never be used in the public reporting of the results of this study. Participation is completely voluntary. If at any point during the [survey, focus group, or interview] your child feels uncomfortable, he or she can stop participation or simply refrain from answering questions. Only researchers will have access to the data, and data will be kept in locked offices on secure computers.

For questions about the [survey, focus group, or interview] please contact [your contact information].

Please mark and return this completed form if you wish or do not wish your child to participate in this research.

Child's name: _____

_____ My child MAY take part in this research

_____ My child MAY NOT take part in this research

Parent/Guardian Signature: _____

Date: _____

Phone Number: _____

While you do not necessarily need IRB approval, it is still important that you have consent from parents.

Third, you must provide informed consent to the subjects of your research. Tools that follow in chapters 4 and 5 (including interview and focus group protocols, as well as a survey template) include directions that provide informed consent. Basically, prior to participation, the subjects of your research should be given a description of the research and its purpose, any foreseeable risks or benefits from participation, its confidentiality, who to contact with questions or concerns, and the voluntary nature of the research. Remember, in every single case, research participants are volunteers and can refuse to participate or end their participation at any time. This is also true for captive populations like a classroom of children or a college fraternity. In no case can you make people participate in research. Of course, you can provide incentives, but if someone wants out, you should simply allow them to walk away from the data collection.

Finally, do not try to deceive your research subjects into believing the needs assessment is about something other than your identified research questions. While in some instances keeping information from research subjects may be important (for example, when comparing the effectiveness of a new pain relief capsule to a placebo), in the case of your community needs assessment, honesty and openness are the best strategies.

If you have further questions or concerns about how to protect the subjects of your research and Institutional Review Boards, visit the website of the U.S. Department of Health and Human Services, Office for Human Research Protection at http://www.hhs.gov/ohrp.

FURTHER READINGS

To learn more about qualitative research and focus groups, consider reading one of the following texts.

Krueger, R., & Casey, M. (2009). *Focus groups: A practical guide for applied research*. Thousand Oaks, CA: Sage Publications.
Stake, R. (2010). *Qualitative research: Studying how things work*. New York: The Guilford Press.

To learn more about quantitative research and developing surveys, consider reading one of the following texts.

Dillman, D. A., Smyth, J. D., & Christian, L. M. (2009) *Internet, mail, and mixed-mode surveys: The tailored design method.* Hoboken, NJ: John Wiley & Sons.
Frankfort-Nachmias, C., & Nachmias, D. (2007). *Research methods in the social sciences.* New York: Worth Publishing.

Collecting Qualitative Data

This chapter provides specific directions for collecting qualitative data through interviews, focus groups, observations, or archives. In chapter 3 you chose one or more data collection methods. The purpose of chapter 4 is to help you actually gather this data. Methods and tools for collection in all four categories of qualitative data appear in this chapter. Use just those you identified in worksheet 4 and feel free to move around in this chapter in order to most efficiently gather your qualitative data. For example, if you chose only focus groups as a qualitative research method, then you don't need to read or work on the interview, observation, or archive sections of the chapter.

TASK 5: COLLECT QUALITATIVE NEEDS ASSESSMENT DATA

By the end of this chapter of the workbook, you will have collected—but not analyzed—data in the form of words that help to answer your research questions. The four sections below provide specific directions for completing this task.

Conducting Interviews with Key Informants

You chose this collection method because you need in-depth knowledge held by a small number of individuals. This necessarily leads to two questions: who are these individuals (the key informants)? and what do I want to know from them? Keep in mind you will be asking key informants to spend some of their valuable time talking to you. You do not want to waste this time, but you also do not want to forget to ask about important details, because it is unlikely that you will have another chance to sit down and ask them. Remember that you are doing research, not political opinion reporting. This means you are an objective observer and chronicler of information. Despite your own concerns over the social issue you are researching, you need to search for unbiased data that will help describe and explain needs. For example, your research question may have to do with the needs of women who are the victims of rape and you are interviewing the local police chief. A poor question would be:

Why don't the police do more to help victims of rape?

While an objective question might be:

Can you please describe the process your department goes through when a rape is reported?

Key informant interviews typically last between 30 and 60 minutes, though I have seen people spend as many as 90 minutes on an interview. However, if you spend longer than that, then you are likely having a discussion beyond the scope of your research. Conduct interviews as professionally as possible and follow these five steps: identify key informants, create an interview protocol, set up a time to meet with informants, conduct the interview, and send thank-you notes to each participant.

Selecting informants is a job for your needs assessment workgroup. The workgroup should search for those individuals who possess in-depth knowledge necessary to answer your research questions. However, you may also need to ask other sources to help identify these informants. In the example from chapter 3, we conducted key informant interviews at the state level in Oregon. The final list of key informants came from three sources. The State Epidemiological Workgroup, the State Advisory Council, and state staff all provided us with a list of names. We looked for the common individuals provided by these groups as well as individuals who represented multiple perspectives. While we knew it was important to have state legislators answer our questions, we also knew that local providers, tribal members, and state staff would have much to say. This large project led to a list of over twenty key informants. You will likely only need to interview between six and ten key informants, and it could be that you have only one or two informants. If your group decides the necessary in-depth information is held by only one person, then maybe you only conduct one interview. However, I would encourage you to think about whom else might have a unique perspective on the issue in order to increase the number of key informants you query. I have also found, after the first ten interviews, the data becomes redundant. Worksheet 5 provides a place for you to identify key informants for interviewing. Create this list in collaboration with your needs assessment workgroup and any other individuals or groups who may be able to identify important informants.

When completing the worksheet, enter the individual's name, position, and the organization he or she represents. This will help you see if you have a good cross-section of perspectives. It will also keep your conversations and interview on a professional level. The final column of the

Worksheet 5. Identify Key Informants for Interviewing

Name and Position	Organization	Contact Information (Phone, E-mail, and Address)

worksheet documents each individual's contact information. This is obviously important for communicating with key informants to set up a time to meet, change scheduling, and send thank-you notes following the interview.

Now that you have identified key informants you must create an interview protocol that provides a road map and questions for the actual interview. This protocol should begin with details of the interview (date, interviewer, and interviewee) and specific instructions for completing the interview. These instructions provide the subject of the interview with informed consent for participation in research. More specifically, it tells him who is conducting the research, the purpose of the research, any potential risks for participating, and that his participation is voluntary. This is followed by a series of structured, semi-structured, or unstructured questions. Tool 2 leads you through the creation of an interview protocol, but first you should practice creating unbiased questions of different types. Exercise 1 provides opportunities to create interview questions around a fictional situation. Complete this exercise to gain experience with composing questions that have nothing to do with your specific needs assessment or research questions.

How did you do? The example questions provided at the end of exercise 1 are in no way the correct answers, just samples of questions I might ask. Note that ten different people will likely write ten different questions. However, all questions should be nonjudgmental and reflect the specific needs assessment research questions.

Now you are ready to create your own interview protocol. Tool 2 provides a template for this protocol. It begins with basic instructions and an introduction to be read to each interviewee. Fill in those areas specific to your research, and then create several questions to obtain unique information and perspectives from each of your identified key informants. Your questions should move from more structured to less structured and hopefully lead to an interview that is more of a discussion than a question-and-answer session. As a practical rule, try to have fewer than ten questions. Make every effort to focus the interview on your research questions. Longer interviews with dozens of questions either lack focus or should be replaced with a survey. Remember, the point of key informant interviews is to obtain in-depth knowledge held by a small number of individuals.

Exercise 1. Practice Writing Interview Questions

A local food cooperative that provides health foods, specialty foods, and locally grown foods to members is considering opening their doors to non-members, but they have no idea what the community needs or wants when it comes to alternatives to local grocery stores. Their needs assessment question is simply, what alternative grocery products does our larger community need? Part of their research includes interviewing several key informants including the current co-op president, a local farmer, the manager of the community's largest supermarket, and the chair of the town's economic development corporation.

In the space below write a structured question (a question that leads to specific values or categories of answers) each of the key informants can respond to.

In the space below write a semi-structured question (a question that leads to short answers but without values or categories) each key informant can respond to.

In the space below write an unstructured question (an open-ended question that leads to deeper discussion) each key informant can respond to.

Examples of each include the following.

Structured: Which type of alternative foodstuff would our community most need? Fruits and Vegetables, Dairy, Bakery, Meat and Seafood, Frozen, or Packaged.

Semi-Structured: Are there specific groups of people in our community that would benefit from the food cooperative opening its doors to non-members?

Unstructured: What advice would you give the food cooperative as it expands its services to non-members?

Once you complete the protocol, show it to colleagues, friends, or members of your workgroup who can provide feedback on how the questions are written and its overall usefulness in answering your research questions. When you feel like the protocol is ready for use, practice conducting an interview on a coworker, friend, or spouse in order to hone your own skills and understand how long the interview will take. Your first experience interviewing should not be with an important key informant.

Now that you have a list of key informants and an interview protocol ready, you must set up times to meet with potential interviewees. Keep this process as professional as possible. You may contact them by phone or e-mail or letter. Think about the norm for their profession (not yours) when deciding how to contact them and request an interview. While you may contact a teenager with a text message, a farmer may prefer a personal request over his fence with a cup of coffee in hand. Members of a university community communicate through e-mail, but an important elected official would likely respond best to a formal letter. It may also be appro-

Tool 2. Interview Protocol

Date: _____

Interviewer Name: _____

Respondent Name: _____

Respondent Title/Position: _____

Respondent Organization: _____

Hello, my name is [name] and I am part of a team [describe who is responsible for research] completing a needs assessment on [research topic]. Thank you for agreeing to participate in this interview. I am interviewing you today because of your knowledge of [research topic]. The purpose of this interview and the needs assessment is to learn more about [paraphrase research question]. The interview will take roughly [minutes], and I hope you will be as open and honest as possible in answering my questions. The risk in participating in this interview is very low and similar to other tasks people do at work or in school. However, your participation in this interview is entirely voluntary. You may choose not to answer any or all of the questions, and you may choose to end this interview at any time. Your answers will be kept confidential, and at no time will your name be publicly attached to data collected through this process. If it is okay with you I will audio record this interview so that I can transcribe what is said exactly and not miss any of your important answers.

Do you have any questions before we start?

Ok, let's begin.

[Questions]

priate to contact others who work for the key informant (like office assistants or schedulers) when the informant holds an important position. You would never call or e-mail a governor or university president directly. Do not be surprised if identified key informants refuse to be interviewed or if you simply cannot get them to commit to a time and place for an interview. In this case, go back to your needs assessment workgroup and discuss another potential interviewee that has similar experiences or knowledge about the subject. For example, you may want to interview the governor of your state and have no luck setting up the meeting, but maybe his chief of staff would be willing to sit down and answer your questions.

Finally, spread the interviews out over at least a week and try not to interview more than one or two individuals in a single day. As you will learn, interviews are hard work and can be exhausting. Give yourself time to catch your breath and consider what you learned from one interview before moving on to the next. Similar to when you requested the interview, you should maintain professionalism at all times as you conduct the interview. Arrive on time and dress at least as nicely as the person you are interviewing. Prepare for the key informant interview the way you might prepare for a job interview with the same person.

Becoming a talented interviewer takes practice, but there is no reason to fear conducting a qualitative interview. While you have a protocol in front of you and may ask some structured questions, the interview itself should be conversational and may drift in many directions. No two interviews using the same protocol will be the same. You want the key informants to tell stories and relate their experiences. Keep in mind, you are not studying the interviewee, you are trying to learn from them. This means the most important skill you possess as an interviewer is to be a good, active listener. Listen not just for the answers but the meaning within those answers.

Yin (2011) reminds interviewers of six helpful hints. First, speak in modest amounts. You should speak much less than the person you are interviewing. They are not trying to learn from you, and you are not trying to interrogate them. Only a few words are necessary when probing for deeper meaning or to keep a conversation moving forward. You will find that most people love talking about themselves, what they know, and their experiences.

Second, be nondirective and flexible. While you will set the boundaries for the conversation and have a sequence of questions in your protocol, allow the interviewee to color the conversation. This means the respondent may move outside your set boundaries or answer questions out of sequence.

Third, stay neutral. Your presentation of self, including your body language, mannerisms, and words, needs to remain impartial and unbiased. As you respond or probe, do not let your own biases and opinions show through. Remember, you are interested in his candid views and not his catered responses to your biases.

Fourth, maintain rapport. You are responsible for avoiding conversations that might harm the other person. This should not be a risky situation for your interviewee. Keep the conversation friendly and remain appreciative of his time and input. One way to build rapport is to reflect your subject's attitudes and emotions. If he is serious you should be serious. If he tells a joke you should laugh. Your goal is to make the key informant feel comfortable enough that he will share his knowledge and experiences with you.

Fifth, use a protocol. You created a protocol above to keep the interview on track. While you want to allow flexibility within the interview, this is also your one chance to get the information. You do not want to arrive back at your office with unanswered questions or missing information. The protocol also allows you to hold something (a prop) during your conversation. This helps the subject know that you are serious about the interview. Of course, it takes practice to find a balance between a nondirective approach and following your protocol.

Sixth, analyze during the interview. Interviewing as a method of data collection is not a passive exercise. You will complete much more data analysis following the completion of all your interviews, but you should also actively analyze the interview as it happens. This means coming up with ideas and jotting them down, probing for deeper meaning during the conversation, and modifying your protocol during the interview if necessary.

You should by now realize that conducting an interview must seem like a natural conversation but will in fact mean a great deal of work. Again, the point of the key informant interview is to gather data, so while you are concentrating on the six above hints, you also have to document what the respondent is telling you. The best ways to do this is to audio record the conversation and then transcribe it later. Digital recorders can be purchased for very little money, and most smartphones now contain audio recording applications. You must inform the subject of your interview that you are recording the conversation (this line appears in the protocol directions in tool 2). Practice with your recording device prior to your first interview to ensure competence in turning it on and off. This may seem simple, but when you get to the interview, you will have many things on your mind and even a simple task can be forgotten.

As a teenager, my American history teacher gave me my first ever interview assignment—talk to an elderly person you know and write down his or her story. I dreaded the task. Both sets of grandparents lived far away, and I didn't really know anyone over the age of about forty. My mother suggested I talk to a neighbor who lived down the street and had long since retired from his job as a music teacher. I went to the interview, old fashioned tape recorder in hand, slowly and without much enthusiasm. I sat down in his living room, promptly forgot to turn on the tape recorder, and began asking questions. Where did you grow up? "Chicago." Can you tell me about it? "I lived in Al Capone's neighborhood," he told me. Then he talked for two hours about Chicago gangsters and the Great Depression and fighting in wars. To this day, I regret not turning on that tape recorder. Do everything in your power to remember to audio record your key informant interviews.

As you exit the interview thank the interviewee for his time and insights. Let him know you will contact him with any further questions or if you need clarification on specific details. When you get back to your office send the interviewee a written thank-you note. This extra step is a very important gesture. The individuals you interview are key informants because they play a major role in the social issue of interest. In all likelihood, you will work with them again or need something else from them. If, following from the example in exercise 1 above, you are completing a needs assessment for a local food cooperative and interviewing the chair of the economic development corporation, then you will likely work with his organization in the future on marketing or a business plan. If you are interviewing a local farmer, then you will likely build a relationship with her to provide produce in the cooperative store. Keep your post-interview correspondence as professional as your pre-interview correspondence—

following the norm for his or her profession. Once you complete all the interviews, you are ready to transcribe and analyze the qualitative interview data. That is the subject of chapter 6.

Conducting Focus Groups

It is possible to conduct key informant interviews with more than one person. Maybe a married couple runs a farm together and you interview both of them sitting at their kitchen table. But when you decide to interview an assembly of local farmers together, it becomes a focus group. You chose focus groups as a data collection method because you need to learn about the shared experiences of a target population. Like interviews, there are steps to follow when gathering focus group data. These include: planning the focus group, creating a focus group protocol, and conducting the focus group itself. Setting up an interview with a key informant is a very simple matter relative to setting up a focus group. Planning makes the difference between a useful, high-quality focus group and a focus group that wastes everyone's time.

In their great book *Focus Groups: A Practical Guide for Applied Research*, Richard A. Krueger and Mary Anne Casey (2009) detail this planning process. They teach us that once you decide to conduct focus groups, you first need to determine whom to study. As always, refer back to your research questions and think about what specific group of individuals can provide a deeper understanding of an issue. Your needs assessment workgroup is critical in choosing target populations. Their input should help you answer two important questions: how many focus groups should you hold, and how should you separate out the potential participants?

I once worked with several communities to hold focus groups around the causes of young adult binge drinking. One community had an economy based on agriculture (wine and fruit mostly) and tourism. They had a large population of young Hispanic men as well as a separate group of young adults of both genders who work in the local service industry. The community felt that one focus group could not provide enough information around the targeted 18- to 25-year-old age group, but how many focus groups should they hold and with whom? Do they separate out the Hispanic population from other young adults? Do they also hold a focus group with older adults, business owners, or law enforcement officers who see and deal with the problem? Another community was home to the large state university. Roughly half of their young adults attended the university, and a significant portion of these students moved to the community from somewhere else to attend the university. The university itself dominated local culture. It was the largest employer in the community and responsible for most social events. Of particular importance were the games of their nationally ranked football team and really any other sporting event. Who do they include in their focus groups? Do they separate students and non-students into different focus groups? Who at the university would be important to include in focus groups? Should they hold a focus group with the parents of students?

Choosing who to focus group is not as simple as just finding any 10 to 12 individuals in your community, but it need not frighten you either. Krueger (1994) writes, "Factors such as geographic location, age, gender, income, participation characteristics, family size, and employment status are all helpful ways to identify who should participate in focus groups" (p. 47). He also advises researchers to remember three categories of particular importance to social service providers—advisory groups, employees, and clients. As always, start with your research questions and work with your needs assessment workgroup to determine who to recruit for participation. Once you decide who to recruit you also have an answer to how many focus groups you should hold. The narrower your research questions the fewer focus groups are necessary. Certainly holding one group is enough if you have a single and simple research question. On the other hand, it may be necessary to hold four or five focus groups. Do not hold more than this, however, because it means that your needs assessment is likely too broad. Also, transcribing and analyzing focus groups can be time-consuming and exhausting. You do not want to lose sight of the purpose of your needs assessment while spending months analyzing ten focus groups. Follow these guidelines for choosing focus group participants.

- Always focus group your target population if possible.
- Conduct more than one focus group with your target population when they represent separate geographies or demographics.

- Divide your target population into multiple focus groups when one subgroup will not feel comfortable speaking or becoming engaged in the presence of another.
- Conduct a focus group with providers of services when they have specialized knowledge of the problem or the target population.
- Conduct a focus group with community stakeholders when they have specialized knowledge of the problem or the target population.

In the example of the community with an economy based upon agriculture and tourism, we held four focus groups. The first was with young Hispanic adults who worked in the agricultural industry. The second and third were with young adult males and young adult females. We separated these men and women into two groups because they had significantly different binge drinking behaviors and potentially different causes for those behaviors. The fourth was with older adults who possessed an understanding of how the community had changed over time.

The next step in the planning process is to decide where and when to hold the focus groups. The location should be easy to find, neutral, private, quiet, and have chairs that can be arranged in a circle. Often during election cycles we see network news programs holding "focus groups" with potential voters to see how a debate influenced their opinions of candidates. A television reporter stands in front of a group of fifteen individuals seated in two or three rows with each row of chairs a little higher than the one in front. All participants face the camera and individually answer questions posed by the reporter. This setup is great for television reporting but awful for a real focus group. One of the most important aspects of a focus group is interaction among participants. It becomes very difficult to interact with others when you are looking at the top of their head or they are seated behind you.

If possible, scout out the location prior to conducting the focus group to make sure it is ideal for group discussion. I have seen focus groups implemented in counseling centers, classrooms, political chambers, libraries, and even the back room of a pizza parlor. All of these locations fit the above criteria and worked well. Depending upon the depth of your research, plan for the focus group to take between 60 and 90 minutes. I have observed shorter focus groups of only 30 to 45 minutes, but you should not keep participants longer than an hour and a half. And schedule the focus groups for times that are most convenient for participants, not for yourself or for your moderator. This might mean a focus group with high school youth takes place right after school, but a focus group with city employees takes place in the evening following their workday. If you plan to conduct more than one focus group in a row, then make sure to plan at least thirty minutes between the two groups to ensure time to recover from the last group and set up for the next.

Worksheet 6 asks you to identify the specific types of individuals to participate in, the location of, and the times for your focus groups. Complete this worksheet with your needs assessment workgroup, and (if it helps) talk to members of your target population to gain their insights into questions of who, where, and when.

The final step in the planning process is to recruit participants from among the specific groups identified in worksheet 6. Some groups of people are easy to find while others can prove much more difficult. When I conducted the focus group with ROTC members mentioned in chapter 3, we simply asked their commanding officer if they could meet with us. He ordered them to show up. However, other groups can be difficult to reach or find for numerous reasons. How difficult would it be to recruit the homeless or individuals with a rare medical condition? A friend of mine conducts focus groups for a medical service company. She often tries to find ten individuals who have received treatment for uncommon medical disorders, and she cannot have access to their medical records or the records of treating physicians. When there are only 200 people with the condition in the entire city, how do you find at least ten to show up to a focus group?

There are four strategies to successfully recruiting focus group participants. First, talk to your target participants. You likely know at least someone who represents the group you want to talk to. Ask them where to find others, what kind of incentives would attract participants, and what might be the most appropriate time and place for the focus group to occur.

Second, offer incentives. Key informants agree to interviews because they are related to their job or something they care about, but focus group

Worksheet 6. Focus Group Plan

Question 1a	Considering your research questions and your community, what population or populations is your needs assessment most interested in?

Question 1b	What subgroups exist within this population?

Question 1c	What reasons are there that subgroups, within the populations you are most interested in, cannot or should not be part of the same group discussion?

Question 1d	What groups of stakeholders or service providers possess specialized knowledge of the populations you are most interested in?

Question 2a	Based upon your answers to questions 1a through 1d, what specific groups will you include in your focus group research?

Question 2b   How many focus groups does this mean you will
                   conduct?

Question 2c   What possible locations within your community would be
                   ideal for your focus groups?

Question 2d   What time of day is most convenient for the specific
                   groups identified in question 2a above?

Summary   Based upon your thoughtful answers above, who will you
                   focus group? Where will the focus groups take place? And
                   when will you conduct the focus groups?

participants usually want to know what they are receiving in return for their time. The more difficult the recruitment, the larger the incentives might need to be. Moreover, make the incentives match the population. Typical incentives for college student participants include coupons to the university bookstore or music downloads. Certainly these would not provide much incentive to the elderly in an assisted living facility or to toddlers in a preschool program.

Third, advertise in places your target group will see. This might include local newspapers, bulletin boards in schools, the back of bathroom stall doors, or in service provider offices. However, be aware that advertising can attract individuals with personal agendas. It is best to combine advertising with purposive selection of participants.

Fourth, get creative. A friend of mine conducted research on the immigrant population of Louisiana following Hurricane Katrina. She wanted to talk with groups of immigrants who were mostly in the United States illegally and, therefore, couldn't receive government help following the disaster. A difficult group to reach. They mostly spoke Spanish only, and no one really knew where they lived. She tried for months to find this unique group and began to think about the one place this population needed to go on a consistent basis—the laundromat. She found her population in a place where they had a good deal of time on their hands as they waited for their laundry to wash and dry, and the result was a fascinating study.

The ideal focus group size is ten individuals. As you recruit, keep in mind that about 20 percent of those who say they are coming will not show up. We even had two ROTC members (ordered by their commanding officer to participate) not show up. This means you should try to get a commitment from 10 to 15 potential participants. If fewer than ten show up, you can still do your research, but fewer than five participants does not make for a focus group. If your recruiting is not going well, then you should consider combining some of the groups identified in worksheet 6. For example, you may want to separate male and female participants into two groups, but it is better to talk to them together if it means having one good focus group rather than two poor focus groups.

Once you decide how many focus groups to conduct, where they will happen, when they will happen, and begin recruiting participants, you need to create a focus group protocol. Similar to an interview protocol, a focus group protocol should reflect your research questions, but the questions are mostly unstructured and designed to elicit group discussion. The focus group is also much less flexible because the moderator needs to maintain order and attention within the group. A typical focus group contains roughly twelve questions that an individual might be able to answer in only a few minutes but a group can discuss at length. Your protocol should create a funnel-down approach to asking questions. This means the questions move from general to specific, with the later questions providing the substance of group discussion. Krueger and Casey (2009) have much to say about writing focus group questions and provide five types of questions in a specific funneling order. These include the following with examples from an alcohol prevention focus group I conducted with resident assistants who worked in university dormitories.

- Opening question. This is a round-robin type question that each participant answers in turn. Design it to be answered quickly and do not expect it to provide answers to your overall research questions; rather, this question makes everyone in the group feel at ease and gets them talking. For example, I know that some of you probably know each other, but I don't know all of you. Could you each tell us your name and one thing that you really love to do on the weekend?

- Introductory question. This question introduces the topic. Write these questions to foster general conversation about the topic and create initial conversation among the participants. For example, what kinds of high-risk drinking do you see in the dormitories or on campus?

- Transition questions. These questions move group conversation toward the main focus of your study, and they set the stage for the productive discussion to come. For example, think back upon when you were college freshmen. What was alcohol use on campus like then?

- Key questions. These are the questions that drive your needs assessment and ultimately answer your research questions. This is also where you want to create real discussion among the participants. Avoid questions that allow for short answers or can be answered with a simple yes or no. For example, what causes high-risk drinking among students who live in the dorms? Or how has drinking behavior on campus changed since you started your jobs as resident assistants?

- Ending questions. These questions bring closure to the discussion and enable participants to look back upon previous comments to summarize their thoughts and ideas. Once again use a round-robin approach, letting each participant speak in turn. For example, if you could say one thing to the president of the university about preventing high-risk drinking on campus what would it be?

Following the questions and discussion, you should summarize some of the things you learned during the focus group and ask participants "Have we missed anything?" Then thank the participants and make sure they receive the incentives they earned. You are now ready to create a focus group protocol. Tool 3 provides the template for this protocol starting with an introduction and rules for the discussion. It leaves blank spaces for you to write in each type of question.

It is time to conduct focus groups. Ideally two people make this happen—one moderates while the other takes notes. Success in this endeavor depends greatly upon the moderator you choose. Often the person who wants to moderate is the worst choice. The moderator should feel at ease in front of groups, but she is not a teacher or presenter. None of the participants show up to learn what the moderator thinks. The best focus groups seem to happen naturally without much moderator interference outside of asking questions. But do not let that fool you; moderators work very hard. According to Krueger and Casey (2009), a moderator should possess the following attributes. She will be familiar with group process and able to exercise control over a group, possess a curiosity about and background knowledge of the subject at hand, be a competent written and oral communicator, make people feel at ease during discussions, have enough self-discipline to hold back her personal opinions and biases, enjoy a warm and friendly manner, and be a genuinely good listener. While the moderator can play many roles in the group discussion (from therapist to referee), I encourage your moderator to be a seeker of

Tool 3. Focus Group Protocol

Hello, my name is [name]. I want to thank you for participating in this group discussion about [research topic]. The purpose of this research is to learn more about [paraphrase research question]. I am audio recording this focus group so that I can transcribe what is said exactly and not miss any of your important answers. I will also take notes on your comments and ideas, but they will be used exclusively for research purposes. Your comments and name will remain confidential and your identity will never be attached to comments or used for publicity or distribution of any kind. If at any point you feel uncomfortable with the discussion or decide not to continue participation in the focus group you are free to leave. The risk of participating in this focus group is very low and similar to other tasks people do at work or in school. Although I am bound to keep your comments confidential, I can't guarantee what you, as individuals, might do after leaving this meeting. To help keep all participants' comments confidential, I ask that when you leave this room you also do not link names to ideas or comments made during this meeting.

Over the next [estimate length] minutes I will ask you a series of questions that lead to discussion, and I hope you will be open and honest in your answers. Before we start, let me remind you of a few ground rules.

- Please, only one person talks at a time.
- No side discussions among participants.
- No one should be put down because of their opinions.
- All of your thoughts and ideas are valued, and there are no right or wrong answers.

Do you have any questions before we start?

Opening Question (round-robin)
[Write a single question that can be answered quickly and helps everyone in the group feel at ease]

Introductory Question
[Write a question that introduces and fosters general conversation about your research topic]

Transition Questions
[Write one or two questions that move group conversation toward the main focus of the needs assessment]

Key Questions
[Write a series of five to ten open-ended questions that create real discussion among participants to answer your research questions]

Ending Question (round-robin)
[Write one question that brings closure to the discussion and allows participants to summarize their ideas]

wisdom. The general attitude is that the group possesses a great deal of important knowledge, and, if asked the right questions, this knowledge will come forth.

Show up to the focus group early, dressed professionally, and with all your tools. These include your protocol, paper and pencil for taking notes, an audio recording device, incentives for participants, and food. Nearly every focus group provides snacks and drinks for participants. I have conducted many focus groups with college students and they simply expect pizza to be available when they show up, but the snacks should reflect your group. Sometimes sandwiches are appropriate. Other times pastry and coffee is expected. I have also seen more healthy alternatives like fruit, vegetables, and bottles of water. In any case, eating tends to promote discussion and camaraderie within a group. Food puts people at ease. Pass out incentives when participants first arrive so if anyone does feel uncomfortable or need to leave, then they are free to do so. Your incentive encourages participation, but it is not a means to lock participants in the room. Do not video record the focus group. While technology has made this easier, video tends to make participants uncomfortable and will not provide information beyond the transcript and your own notes. Finally, be respectful of the time. Allow a small amount of time at the beginning for individuals to show up and engage in small talk, but start promptly. Then finish within the allotted time. Once completed, you are ready to transcribe and analyze your focus group data. Again, chapter 6 addresses this next step.

DEMONSTRATION 3: THE PORK FOCUS GROUP

As a graduate student, I had the opportunity in classes and as part of various research projects to facilitate focus groups. One day I saw an advertisement in the local newspaper for a marketing company in need of focus group participants and realized I had never before been on the participant side of a focus group. Participation also came with an incentive, so I quickly signed up and was chosen. Only upon reaching the designated location at the appropriate time did I learn what we would be discussing—pork! The incentive was a $30 gift certificate for pork products redeemable at any local grocer.

While I waited for others to show up and group discussion to start, I opened a book and began an assigned reading for one of my graduate seminars. The moderator (a middle-aged woman dressed in a skirt and suit jacket and wearing heels) interrupted me with a rather mundane question. "And Rodney, what are your plans for the weekend?" I looked up, slightly irritated because I had a reading assignment due the next day, and it was not yet time to begin the focus group. "Joe here is leaving for vacation, and Susan's daughter is turning four years old." Why was this woman bothering me with small talk before the discussion of pork had even begun? I was busy. Then it dawned on me. We had begun, and this woman was a real pro. She had quickly identified a participant who was not yet engaged and posed a threat to group discussion. The next ninety minutes unfolded like spring training for focus group facilitators. The moderator had us laughing and sharing and discussing pork as if it were the most important issue in the world.

To start, there were ten of us men and women in the room, sitting comfortably around a big, but not dominating, table. We clearly represented a target population of young married people with small children. There were drinks and pastries provided, but surprisingly no pork. The moderator's assistant almost invisibly took notes and audio recorded the discussion. We started with small talk until we felt comfortable and then began a general discussion about eating pork. What is our favorite cut of pork? How often do we enjoy pork? Do we eat pork at home or just in restaurants? Then we moved to more specific and direct questions about our fears around preparing pork and its potential health risks. We finished with ideas on how to better spread the message that pork can be healthy, delicious, and safe. I remained stoic throughout because to this day my family rarely eats pork. I expressed my concerns over trichinosis (the result of a college major in microbiology) and how every time I barbequed pork chops they became hockey pucks (the result of me grilling everything over high heat). Then the moderator brought up barbequed ribs. Somehow it never occurred to me that the delicious ribs at my favorite new local restaurant were pork. My participation in the focus group increased dramatically. In the end, I learned a great deal from a talented moderator even though the topic had nothing at all to do with my social service interests.

MAKING QUALITATIVE OBSERVATIONS

You may have chosen qualitative observation as a way to collect data because you need data unfiltered by key informants or other members of the community. When observing, you are the data collection instrument, so remain aware that your role (or the role of volunteer observers) is to document with words the answers to your research questions. However, recently and with the ubiquity of digital images, observation may take other forms as well. Most common among these are photographs of what you observe. For example, you may describe in words posters for bands that cover downtown street lampposts, or you may just take a picture of the posts themselves. The process of using images for observational research has become known as digital storytelling and is described in more detail below. Regardless of how you observe, much thought needs to go into the observation process. Like conducting interviews or focus groups, observation follows several logical steps. Start by answering a number of questions and end by creating an observational protocol. What will be observed? Who will observe it? Where will they observe it? When will they observe it? Will they play the role of passive observer or participant? Of course, the answers to all these queries depend upon your needs assessment research questions, and think of the resulting product of your qualitative observational research as a story of need.

Note that this section on the collection of qualitative observation data is very similar to the section on the collection of quantitative observation data in chapter 5. However, while the methodology is comparable, qualitative observation leads to a story told in words and quantitative observation leads to descriptive numbers. If you are working through both sections, then consider how they might be completed more efficiently together.

Let us begin with the first question (what will we observe?), using the example of a needs assessment for a youth baseball league. Assume the main research question is something like, what does our community baseball program need to increase participation and foster excellence? If we chose observation as a research method, then it seems fairly obvious we will want to attend some of the baseball practices and games. We may also want to look more closely at the equipment and fields used for these games and practices. Now consider your needs assessment and the social issues it is concerned with. Where is the "game" being played? Where will you see people playing it? What equipment are they using? For example, you may be interested in downtown vandalism. Where is vandalism happening? Who do we believe is doing it? When is it happening? What are people using to vandalize the downtown? If you can answer these questions, then you can answer the question of what will be observed. Keep in mind, however, that your own safety is more important than any observational research. A researcher would never sit and take notes next to a pitcher during a baseball game. Similarly, you would never try to catch criminals in the act or peer through windows at a domestic violence situation.

Once you understand what to observe, you need to decide who will observe it. Like a good interviewer or focus group moderator, quality observation takes practice. While being good at the former means active listening, being a good observer means active watching. Think of yourself as a detective who is documenting the scene of a crime. How is the activity unfolding? Who is involved? How are people behaving and reacting? What in the environment is affecting the situation? More specifically, you need to find a volunteer who can spend a good deal of time observing. In the case of the youth baseball league, we may have parents on our needs assessment workgroup who already attend many practices and games and could play the role of active observer. You may also choose to have more than one individual observe and then later compare responses looking for consensus around answers to the research questions.

Once you decide what to observe and who will observe it, answering the next two questions should be straightforward. Choose where and when to observe based upon the most likely place and time to see the best example of the social issue you are interested in. For the youth baseball league that might mean formal games and informal practices, but what if a team is playing out of town against a team from another league? What if the program we are interested in has multiple fields to play on? Again, choose to observe at a place and time that provide the best example of what you are interested in. If your needs assessment has to do with problem gambling behavior, you may choose to send a couple of observers into a local casino. Where in that casino and when might they be most likely to see individuals with gambling problems? Also, casinos tend to be open twenty-four hours a day and your observers cannot be there all day every day. So, how much observation is enough observation? Certainly baseball games are limited to a certain number of innings (seven in most youth baseball leagues), but other situations might not be as easily defined. Observation for your needs assessment takes place in hours, not days. You may want to attend multiple events or travel to multiple locations, and you may want to observe on different days at different times. As always, make these decisions based upon answering your needs assessment research questions.

Finally, consider whether you will be a participant observer or passive observer. Both have advantages and disadvantages, but being a passive observer is most common. Here is the difference using the youth baseball example. Parents relaxing in the stands, a volunteer who sits at the edge of the park watching practice, and a researcher who walks around the stadium watching both the game and people interacting with the game are potential passive observers. The coach on the field, the player at first base, and a parent keeping score on the bench are potential participant observers. Participant observers are part of the game and may even affect the outcome of the game. Passive observers simply watch the game unfold. In a social service situation this can be seen the same way. A school resource officer may participate on your needs assessment workgroup and play the role of participant observer of needs within the school where she works. On the other hand, you may choose a passive observer who has little knowledge of or any connection to the school. The major plus for participant observation is that no one knows and understands a situation like an actual participant. However, taking notes and documenting the situation while participating can be very difficult, and participant observers can often lack objectivity. A player who strikes out each time he comes to the plate will be more inclined to see the need for new bats than someone from the outside. The major plus for passive observers is objectivity and the luxury to observe and document at the same time.

Before we create a plan or protocol I want to provide you with a way to practice observation. Exercise 2 asks you to observe people recreating in a local park.

How did you do? Was it harder or easier than you thought it would be? Would it be nice to have some photographs of the things you observed? This is exactly what researchers began to think about observation as part of needs assessment in the 1990s. Caroline C. Wang and Mary Ann Burris were working in China when they created what is known as Photovoice

Exercise 2. Practice Qualitative Observing

For this exercise, pretend you are working on a needs assessment for the local Parks and Recreation Department. The research question is, how can we make our parks more attractive for the public in order to increase the number of people who use them? Part of this research involves observing the environment and use of local parks. To complete this exercise, plan to spend at least one hour at one local park taking notes, walking around and through the park, and sitting quietly watching people. Do this during a pleasant afternoon or evening when people are most likely to use the park. Your goal is to tell the story of how and why people use the park without talking to anyone. Remember you are the research instrument. As you sit and walk around your chosen park, take notes on the following.

What is the general atmosphere or environment of the park?

What kinds of recreational opportunities does the park provide?

What kinds of people visit the park?

What kinds of activities are they participating in?

How long do people tend to visit the park?

What parts of the park are most and least often used?

Where do people congregate?

Where do people avoid going?

as a way to allow rural women to impact the politics and services that most affected them. Photovoice is a variant of digital storytelling, a research method that takes advantage of how commonplace photographs, videos, and audio recordings have become. Unlike just taking a camera with you when you observe, Photovoice puts the camera in the hands of your target population. Wang and Burris (1994) gave disenfranchised women in rural China cameras with film and then later developed the film for the project. Today with smartphones and other devices, you or your target population can easily and quickly document need through photographs, video, or audio.

However, you cannot take pictures or record individuals without their permission. Crowd scenes are one thing, but if individuals can be easily identified you need permission. This is especially true for children. But many times you will not need photos of individuals to tell your story. Also, keep in mind that Photovoice as a needs assessment tool is much more than simply taking pictures. It is a way to empower your target population while systematically collecting observational data, and it comes with a specific and rigorous methodology. This includes the following steps.

First, understand and define the problem to observe. This is important because you do not want to send observers into the field with no direction, but since you are conducting a community needs assessment you should already have done this.

Second, train the observers. They need to know the major theme of the observation, questions you are trying to answer, and how to use their cameras/phones to take pictures. They also need to understand how and where to send those photographs.

Third, you need to facilitate a group discussion about all the photos with your observers following their observations. The goal of this discussion is critical reflection and involves choosing the photographs that best and most accurately reflect the need or concern, tell the story of need, and identify themes of need. In sum, the point of Photovoice is to allow the target population of your services to provide observational input.

Much easier is for you or other observers from your needs assessment workgroup to take photos as part of observational data collection. This is in addition to the notes and journal keeping you will already do. In practice, returning to the youth baseball league example, you may add photographs of baseball practices, games, equipment, and the field to your observations. Or you may ask the players and the coaches to take photographs of what they perceive as important about the league. Again, your research questions should drive all the digital images collected as observational data.

You are ready to make some decisions and create a plan for observation. Worksheet 7 asks you to detail the what, who, when, where, and how questions about your qualitative observational research.

Now that you have a plan for qualitative observations, you need to create an observational protocol. This protocol provides structure to the observation and a place to take notes. It also provides direction to any digital documentation you may put into action. Remember the goal of your observation is to tell a story. Tool 3 provides a template for completing your observation and taking notes. It assumes you or other volunteers (who might be part of the target population) may take photographs, but it does not provide for a Photovoice analysis. If you want to go a step further and include Photovoice in your needs assessment, I encourage you to adapt this protocol and read more about Photovoice.

Key for creating this protocol is deciding upon major themes and questions. Tool 4 provides one column with multiple cells to write down theme questions and a second column for note taking. Similar to exercise 2 above, your theme questions should be open-ended and focus your observations in a way that answers your overall research questions and leads you to capture the story of what you observe. For example, what kinds of vandalism is taking place downtown? There are rows enough to ask three theme questions and a place to document digital observations. Of course, you should feel free to add rows for more questions if necessary and do not need to ask three if fewer will do. If you do feel the need to ask more than five questions around observation, then consider how focused your needs assessment is. Surely, having ten or more theme questions means you are asking with too much detail or your needs assessment is too broad.

It is time to implement your observation plan either alone, in pairs, or with multiple individuals. Once completed, you are ready to transcribe and analyze your qualitative observations as described in chapter 6.

Worksheet 7. Qualitative Observation Plan

Question 1a	Considering your research questions and your community, describe what you will observe for your needs assessment. In other words, what "game" are you interested in observing?
Question 1b	Who will be conducting the observations? Will there be one individual observer or more than one? Will you utilize your target population as observers?
Question 1c	Where and when will the observations take place?
Question 1d	Would participant observation or passive observation provide the best information for answering your research questions?
Question 1e	Is it appropriate to use digital storytelling? If so, what kind will you use?

Summary   Based upon your thoughtful answers above, provide the
               following:

               What will be observed?

               Who will observe it?

               When will they observe it?

               Where will they observe it?

               Will they participate in it?

Using Qualitative Archives

You chose this final type of qualitative data collection because you need
or have historical, organizational, or readily available information that
does not require original research. Remember, these are not numbers like
the percentage of youth smoking cigarettes or the number of single parent
households; rather, this data is in the form of lists, journal entries, stories,
old photographs, meeting minutes, and more. And this can mean mountains of information. My five-step plan for you to manage it includes
brainstorming, inventorying, prioritizing, grouping, and filing. Similar to
a funnel, these steps will help you identify the universe of possibilities
and narrow it to a reasonable and targeted amount of data. As always,
your research questions drive the process.

   Let us start with brainstorming. This term was made popular by
advertising executive Alex Faickney Osborn in his 1963 book *Applied
Imagination*. Osborn's method focused on a quantity of ideas while withholding criticism of these ideas and encouraging unusual and creative

Tool 4. Qualitative Observation Protocol

Date:

Time:

Place:

Observer Name:

Theme Questions	Notes and Observations
1.	
Were digital observations made? By whom and of what?	

Theme Questions	Notes and Observations
2.	
Were digital observations made? By whom and of what?	

Theme Questions	Notes and Observations
3.	
Were digital observations made? By whom and of what?	

thoughts. Today brainstorming is commonly used in many organizations to stimulate ideas or lists in a (hopefully) safe environment. However, some research has shown group brainstorming can be less effective than individuals working alone (Stroeb, Diehl, & Abakoumkin, 1992). For this reason, I want you to begin to inventory all potential qualitative archives through a guided brainstorming process. This process includes three specific questions asked of the group and of individuals: what possible qualitative archives exist? Who else might help identify archival sources? And what criteria will be used to narrow these sources? Notice that I mentioned groups and individuals. The brainstorming process should begin with your needs assessment workgroup or a subsection of that group but move to individuals in two important ways.

First, you should offer members of the brainstorming group the opportunity to provide ideas even after the group meets. Second, the group will identify other individuals who can provide further archival data sources (hence the second question above). Worksheet 8 provides a simple protocol for brainstorming. Feel free to take notes on this worksheet, on scratch paper, or electronically. Remember, all thoughts are valuable, and this is not the place to criticize or eliminate ideas. The end goal of this exercise is to inventory all the possible sources of archival data.

Worksheet 8. Brainstorming Qualitative Archives

Questions	Notes
What possible sources of qualitative data exist?	
Who else might know of other sources of qualitative archives?	
What criteria will you use to narrow the list of archives to just those that answer your research questions?	

Notice too, the final question begins the prioritizing process. Narrowing criteria should reflect your research questions and your need for high-quality data. For example, you may narrow based upon how old the data is, the quality of the information, or its availability.

Once you complete brainstorming within the group and individually, you have lists of potential data sources. Putting these together in a formal document or electronic spreadsheet provides an inventory of these sources. This inventorying leads naturally to the prioritizing and grouping of data. Create this list without bias because it should come close to representing the universe of possible and relevant archives. Once your inventory is complete, you can apply your criteria with the express goal of keeping or eliminating data sources. For example, if one criterion is to reject any data more than five years old, then you would eliminate board meeting minutes from the creation of an organization in 1994, but keep recent posts to the organization's website. This prioritized inventory need not be huge because the data must answer your research questions, and you will ultimately end up analyzing all of it.

Working alone or with your needs assessment workgroup, place the remaining data sources into groups. This will help organize your thoughts and prepare you for later analysis. These groups will likely appear naturally. For example, you may have several archives sorted into historical photographs, participant information, and board activities. Following prioritization, you may also only end up with a single useful archival data source. Consider the number of other types of data you are collecting overall, and find a balance with the qualitative archives you use.

You should now have a parsimonious list of archival data sources. This is not the same as actually having the data. The final step is to collect the data from these sources and place them into physical or electronic folders. This filing process should represent the groupings you created above, though a single grouping might require one physical and one electronic folder. Photographs, for instance, may exist electronically and on pieces of paper in photo albums. You may find yourself eliminating data sources in this final step as you realize some things are not truly accessible. In the end, you will have a small collection of qualitative archives ready for the analysis described in chapter 6. Tool 5 below provides a place to document this process. Use it to record each step leading to your useful archives.

Tool 5. Qualitative Archives

Process	Notes and Lists
Inventory of possible qualitative archival data sources	
Prioritization criteria	
Prioritized inventory of qualitative archival data sources	
Groupings of qualitative archival data sources	
List of physical files	
List of electronic files	

The process for collecting qualitative archives is nearly identical to that for collecting quantitative archives. If you decide to collect both, then you should adapt the process to accomplish both together.

DEMONSTRATION 4: A CHILDREN'S MUSEUM

A children's museum in a medium-sized suburb conducted a needs assessment based upon two research questions. How can we better serve the children in our community? Should we build a new facility? The museum operated out of a historic old home in the corner of a local park. It contained numerous history and science exhibits that provided hands-on experiences for school-aged youth. The museum also offered numerous science, nature, art, and craft classes for children of all ages. The board recently hired a new director who really wanted to make changes, but before doing so she sought quality information on the needs of their museum and clientele. Their needs assessment plan involved a community survey, focus groups with kids and parents, and qualitative archival data. The new director figured this final data type provided easily accessible information worth investigating. She pulled together interested board and staff members to brainstorm potential archival data sources. The brainstorming led to the following potential qualitative archives.

- Newspaper articles
- Children's museum website
- Meeting minutes
- Photographs of the historical house the museum now occupies
- Past brochures listing services and classes
- Comment cards from the suggestion box
- Comments posted on the website
- A book on the history of the town
- Staff performance evaluations
- Written interpretations of annual financial reports
- A local television news report about the museum
- Written descriptions of museum exhibits and hands-on activities
- Personal web-based entries by current and past staff members

- Photographs of children using the museum exhibits and classes
- Stories children wrote in the museum's young author class
- Results of an exit interview with the museum director who recently resigned his position

They also identified the following individuals who might have more ideas for finding qualitative archives: the recently resigned director who served in that position for five years, the pottery teacher who has worked at the museum since its opening, two parents who started the museum nearly twenty years earlier, and the director of the town's historical society. These individuals identified a few more potential sources.

- Children's art and science projects
- The museum mission and vision statement
- The application for the building to be placed on the National Registry of Historic Places

The brainstorming group also decided upon two narrowing criteria. They only wanted to consider archival data that reflected children who use the museum or described the history and importance of the building itself. This prioritization led to six sources of qualitative archives.

- Comment cards from the suggestion box
- Photographs of children using the museum exhibits and classes
- Stories children wrote in the museum's young author class
- Children's art and science projects
- The application for the building to be placed on the National Registry of Historic Places
- Photographs of the historical house the museum now occupies

These sources were separated into two groups and then collected mirroring the narrowing criteria. The first four sets of data were gathered together and placed in a box labeled "qualitative data from our users." Of course, they only chose a recent selection of art and science projects because of the sheer volume created each year. They also stored an electronic copy of the application for the National Registry of Historic Places and dozens of digital photos of the historical house in a computer folder labeled "qualitative data about our building."

Depending upon the types of qualitative data you chose to collect in chapter 3 and then pursue in this chapter, you should now have a collection of interviews, focus groups, observations, or archives ready to analyze. In chapter 5, we will add to that collection by gathering quantitative data.

FURTHER READINGS

To learn more about collecting qualitative data, consider reading one of the following texts.

Krueger, R., & Casey, M. (2009). *Focus groups: A practical guide for applied research.* Thousand Oaks, CA: Sage Publications.
Stake, R. (2010). *Qualitative research: Studying how things work.* New York: Guilford Press.

To learn more about Photovoice as a needs assessment and qualitative research tool, visit the website dedicated to this interesting new type of research at http://www.photovoice.org.

Collecting Quantitative Data

This chapter provides specific directions for collecting quantitative data through surveys, observations, or archives. In chapter 3, you chose one or more data collection methods. The purpose of chapter 5 is to help you actually gather this data. Methods and tools for collection in all three categories of quantitative data appear in this chapter. Use just those you identified in worksheet 4 and feel free to move around in this chapter in order to most efficiently gather your quantitative data. For example, if you chose only archives as a quantitative research method, then you don't need to read or work on the survey or observation sections of the chapter.

TASK 6: COLLECT QUANTITATIVE NEEDS ASSESSMENT DATA

By the end of this chapter of the workbook, you should have collected— but not yet analyzed—data in the form of numbers that help to answer your research questions. The three sections below provide specific directions for completing this task.

Creating and Implementing Surveys

Many in the social service field think of needs assessment as synonymous with doing a survey. During a recent project, I led nearly twenty subrecipient communities through a needs assessment process that provided data from dozens of sources and methodology for making decisions with local coalitions based upon documented need. By all accounts, the work was time-consuming and difficult. It involved many of the data collection techniques discussed here, including searches for archival data and conducting focus groups and interviews. It was very comprehensive, but it did not include original surveys of any kind. When they were finished (and despite my warnings), nearly half of the communities implemented some kind of survey of their own anyway. These were all poorly done, and I could not do anything to stop them. One community asked questions using a five-point scale. Instead of providing places to mark "strongly agree," "agree," "disagree," and so on, they told respondents to place certain numbers in spaces following the questions (a practice neither I nor the respondents had ever seen). Nearly every respondent made random checkmarks instead of writing appropriate numbers, providing no useful information. Another community actually used the questions from our provided focus group protocol as their survey instrument. I hope you realize from working through this book how inappropriate that might be because of the very different methods that are focus groups and surveys. Every community that created their own survey chose an entirely biased sample of respondents.

Do not misunderstand me. Surveys can be a wonderful way to understand community need, but gathering quality survey data is difficult and often requires more resources than other data collection efforts. If you chose a survey as a way to collect quantitative data, then this section provides the guidance to do an effective job of creating and implementing this survey. I will walk you through the process of writing a survey, choosing a practical sample that best represents your community, and finally implementing the survey in a timely manner. Experience has shown me there are more poor surveys in the world than good ones. My goal for you is to collect the highest-quality, most useful survey data possible, making your survey one of the good ones.

Survey research requires three critical steps. First, you need to create a well written, logical survey instrument which avoids the many pitfalls of poorly written surveys. For example, I recently borrowed questions from a national survey on mental health and substance use. Numerous questions contain the phrase "a lot." As in "I drank a lot of alcohol," or "I spent a lot of money on alcohol last month." Of course the measure "a lot" is incredibly subjective. As we create your survey instrument, I will teach you to avoid poor questions and create useful and specific measures.

Second, you must draw a representative sample of your population. In nearly every case, you will use the survey to draw conclusions about your community. This means the sample of people must represent your community. This is an area where many in the social service field fail. They survey people at the health fair, who walk in the front door, or who are willing to take the survey at a local event. These samples are convenient but usually don't represent the population of interest very well.

Third, you need to implement the survey as efficiently and prudently as possible. There are four ways to survey people: over the telephone, through the mail, on the Internet, or in person. Of course, you can use a combination of these methods, and which you choose depends much upon your sample. You also want to make sure to have the largest completion rate possible. This refers to the percentage of those you ask to take surveys who actually answer all or most of the survey questions.

Writing Survey Questions

The foundation of any survey is its questions. This means you must construct high-quality questions rather than those Salkind (2012) calls "absolutely terrible." Specific questions to avoid include:

- Those a respondent cannot answer based upon their knowledge. Which political party in Burundi do you believe should control the national government?
- Those with double negatives. Do you never not smoke cigarettes?
- Those that actually ask two questions at once. Do you enjoy shooting rifles and handguns?
- Those that people are unlikely to answer honestly. How often is it okay to kick puppies?
- Those that lead respondents to answer in a particular way. Would you vote for Joe Johnson if you knew he hated baby animals?

The questions you construct should be clear, understandable, easy to answer, and elicit responses from each person surveyed. You also want to collect accurate information while decreasing the burden on each survey respondent. With this in mind, you will only construct close-ended questions for your needs assessment survey because you are collecting quantitative data here. These fall into two groups: questions with ordered response categories and questions with unordered response categories. The difference becomes very important in chapter 7 when we analyze your quantitative data. You should also collect demographic data on your survey. Questions with ordered response categories elicit a yes/no or scaled response. Here is an example from chapter 3.

How safe is the community where you live?

_____ very unsafe

_____ somewhat unsafe

_____ somewhat safe

_____ very safe

Notice that these responses can be ordered. Feeling "very safe" reflects a greater feeling of safety than feeling "somewhat safe." Similarly, a question with only two categories can be ordered. Here is an example of one of these questions that has been asked for decades:

Do you approve or disapprove of the way [put President's name here] is handling his job as President?

_____ approve

_____ disapprove

The reason we consider this a question with ordered response categories (even though the answer is dichotomous) is because responding with "approve" reflects a greater amount of approval than responding with "disapprove." The same is true for a yes/no question. Responding "yes" reflects a greater amount of agreement than responding "no."

One specific type of ordered response category is the rating scale. Often considered synonymous with a Likert scale, rating scales provide ordered and mutually exclusive responses that appear along a range. Of course, the safe community question above is a rating scale. You have probably most often seen a five-point scale in a question like this.

To what extent do you favor or oppose raising the sales tax by one cent in our county?

_____ strongly favor

_____ somewhat favor

_____ neither favor nor oppose

_____ somewhat oppose

_____ strongly oppose

Researchers often expand questions like this to seven points, but a five-point scale is most common. Use seven-point scales when you need more detail or when the response you are looking for is less about feelings or attitudes and more about quality or characteristics. For example, you might use a seven-point scale when considering the quality of a product (where 1 is the lowest possible quality and 7 is the highest possible quality). Moreover, most people are familiar with the phrase "on a scale from one to ten." I have even seen political surveys use scales from 1 to 100. These are called feeling thermometers, and there may be reasons for using them based upon future analysis. However, my experience has been that respondents rarely answer with a 43 or 67; rather, they answer with numbers ending in five or zero, making it a 10- or 20-point scale in the end. Dillman (2007) lists six good scalar concepts for our use. These include strongly agree to strongly disagree, very favorable to very unfavorable, excellent to poor, extremely satisfied to extremely dissatisfied, high priority to low priority, and a complete success to a complete failure. Keep these in mind later as you create a survey tool.

When it comes to data analysis, questions with ordered response categories are typically more interesting than those without. However, not everything you need to know can be ordered. Questions with unordered response categories elicit a preference or preferences among a set of choices. Here is a simple example.

Do you own or rent your home?

_____ own

_____ rent

These questions become slightly more complicated as you add more choices. Choices should be mutually exclusive—meaning the response categories don't overlap. And they should be exhaustive—meaning the response categories cover all possible answers. Here is an example of a simple question with many unordered response categories.

> Of the six subject areas listed below, which was your favorite when you were in high school?
>
> _____ math
> _____ science
> _____ art
> _____ English
> _____ physical education
> _____ history

Often researchers add an "other" category at the end with a line offering a space for respondents to write some other response, but I discourage you to do this in your needs assessment because conducting analysis, making comparisons, and drawing conclusions become more difficult. Another convention of unordered response categories is the "mark all that apply" question. Again, I discourage you from using this type of question because they can be difficult to analyze and because bias and other analysis problems may occur (Dillman, 2007). While some researchers make all that apply categories useful and appropriate, we will avoid these in your needs assessment survey to keep it simple and straightforward, while best answering your research questions.

Finally, your survey should contain demographic items. These can have either ordered (like household income) or unordered (like race and ethnicity) response categories. The survey tool below provides the accepted ways to ask demographic questions and allows you to choose which demographics are important to ask on your survey. Remember, demographics offer more than descriptions of your respondents. The real power of demographics is to know how different groups (men versus women or older versus younger people) answer different questions. This might allow you to better understand the needs of various populations in your community.

For instance, men prefer attending sporting events while women prefer attending cultural events, or parents between the ages of 18 and 25 are most likely to use the local food bank.

Exercise 3 below gives you the opportunity to practice writing survey questions, but before you complete the exercise, let me give you one last piece of advice. No professional survey research center would be without Dillman, Smyth, and Christian's book *Internet, Mail, and Mixed-Mode Surveys: The Tailored Design Method.* In the book, the authors share their principles for writing survey questions. Keep many of these in mind as you practice writing questions or as you construct your own survey (Dillman, Smyth, & Christian, 2009).

- Choose simple over specialized words.
- Choose as few words as possible to pose the question.
- Use complete sentences to ask questions.
- Avoid vague qualifiers when more precise estimates can be obtained.
- Eliminate check-all-that-apply question formats.
- Develop response categories that are mutually exclusive.
- Be sure each question is technically accurate.
- Avoid asking respondents to say yes in order to mean no.
- Avoid double-barreled questions.
- Soften the impact of potentially objectionable questions.
- Avoid asking respondents to make unnecessary calculations.

I will not spend pages here describing the detail of each, but if you do have questions find any edition of Dillman, Smyth, and Christian's book for further information. In general, write straightforward, easy-to-answer questions. Questions should not lead respondents to answer the way you want them too; instead, questions should provide an accurate picture of respondent qualities, attitudes, beliefs, feelings, and behaviors.

How did you do? Writing quality survey questions can be difficult. For this reason, we often use suitable questions that come from other surveys. If your needs assessment requires information that is also collected at a national or state level, then survey questions likely already

Exercise 3. Practice Writing Survey Questions

Returning to the example from Exercise 1, a local food cooperative that provides health foods, specialty foods, and locally grown foods to members is considering opening their doors to non-members, but they have no idea what the community needs or wants when it comes to alternatives to local grocery stores. Their needs assessment question is simply, what alternative grocery products does our larger community need? As part of the needs assessment, they plan to survey a large sample of citizens from all parts of the community. For this exercise, write only close-ended questions.

In the space below, create a survey question with ordered response categories that create a rating scale and would provide useful information to the food cooperative. Choose an appropriate five-point scalar concept.

In the space below, create a survey question that requires a yes or no response and would provide useful information to the food cooperative.

In the space below, create a survey question with unordered response categories that require a respondent to choose one preference among several choices and would provide useful information to the food cooperative.

Examples of each include the following.

Rating scale question:

To what extent do you favor or oppose the local food cooperative expanding its services to non-members?

_____ strongly favor

_____ favor

_____ neither favor nor oppose

_____ oppose

_____ strongly oppose

Yes or no question:

If the local food cooperative no longer required a membership to buy food, would you shop there for groceries?

_____ yes

_____ no

Preference question:

Which one type of alternative foodstuff would you most prefer to buy at the local food cooperative?

_____ fruits and vegetables

_____ dairy

_____ bakery

_____ meat and seafood

_____ frozen

_____ packaged

exist for your use. For example, there is no need to rewrite or come up with your own questions on youth alcohol use. Standard ways to ask this question already exist on surveys like Monitoring the Future or the Youth Risk Behavior Survey. The benefit of using existing questions is researchers have already vetted, tested, and improved them.

This also means questions should be valid and reliable—two things you should aim for when creating your questions. Validity refers to a question (any data you collect really) measuring what it intends to measure. Does the question you ask young people about their alcohol use actually measure underage drinking? Reliability refers to a question (again, any data you might collect) consistently measuring something the same way. Will the question you ask young people about their alcohol use get the same answers from the same person over and over again? Think of your survey as a dartboard. Validity means that your measure is hitting the bull's-eye; reliability means that your measure is hitting the same place on the board every time. Ideally, your questions will hit the bull's-eye over and over.

The best way to ensure validity and reliability is to use questions previously created and tested by other researchers. However, this doesn't mean any question you see on a survey is valid and reliable. There are statistical techniques for ensuring both, but they are beyond the scope of this workbook. Testing for reliability necessarily means using a measure multiple times. Testing for validity can be done in a number of ways, but most common and useful for you is something called face validity (Welch & Comer, 2006). This relies upon your subjective assessment of the measure. On its face is your question a good measure of what you are trying to learn? At this point I only want you to be aware of these issues as you move forward with writing survey questions and constructing a survey instrument. If you consider validity, reliability, and the above principles, then you will end up with a quality instrument.

Ponder two more factors before actually constructing your survey tool. First, I have not covered the exhaustive variety of ways we can ask survey questions, but I do want to discuss how the scalar questions described above can be turned into indices. An index is useful if you are trying to understand an overall attitude or belief. These are not useful for factual information; instead, they are used for collecting data on how people think or feel. For example, a single question might tell you if a young person used alcohol or drugs in the past month, but an index can tell you about his overall attitude toward drug use. Indices are created by summing the responses to multiple scalar questions. Youth attitude toward drug use is typically measured by asking:

> How wrong do you think it is for someone your age to . . .
>
> Drink beer, wine, or hard liquor regularly?
>
> Smoke cigarettes?
>
> Use chewing tobacco?
>
> Smoke marijuana?
>
> Use LSD, cocaine, amphetamines, or another illegal drug?

Ordered response categories include very wrong, wrong, a little bit wrong, and not wrong at all (Arthur, Hawkins, Pollard, Catalano, & Baglioni, 2002). The responses to each of the five substance types (scored 1 to 4) are added together to create an index of how a young person generally feels about using drugs—his attitude toward drug use. If a respondent answered very wrong to every question, his score would be the sum of five 1's. If a respondent answered not wrong at all to every question, his score would be the sum of five 4's. The index ranges from 5 to 20, but you can average the final score to create a final attitude toward drug use score that reflects the original response categories. I will discuss this more in chapter 7 when you learn about the analysis of quantitative data. For now consider creating an index in your survey if you want to understand the overall feelings or attitudes of your respondents.

Second, while creating quality questions is a tremendously important part of constructing a survey, you also need to pay attention to the order in which you ask those questions. There are nearly as many ways to order survey questions as there are ways to write them. For your needs assessment, start with an introduction and directions for completing the survey, then move on to the most interesting questions first in order to stimulate curiosity, followed by the most threatening questions, and finishing with demographics. Put demographics last because they are the least important and least exciting of the questions. Threatening questions are those that are most likely to make a respondent stop taking the survey. By placing them near the end we increase the likelihood that a respondent will at least answer some of the questions if not all. Also try to funnel the questions from general to more specific (think about how focus groups follow a funnel-down approach), as well as keeping the survey as logical as possible. For instance, you want to place a general question about what religion someone is prior to a question about church attendance. Only after these would you ask questions about specific devotional practices. In a recent survey on adult alcohol use, we began with the question, have you used alcohol in the past twelve months? For those people that answered yes, we followed this with questions about drinking and driving and other risky behaviors. The first question is clearly a screening question because we were mostly interested in behaviors of respondents who actually drink alcohol. If someone answered the first question with no, then we would not ask them the following questions. It would not make logical sense to place a question about whether or not someone had used alcohol in the past twelve months after questions about risky drinking behavior.

Creating a Survey Tool

Now you are ready to construct a survey tool for your needs assessment. When written well, responses to this tool will provide answers to your specific needs assessment research questions. Tool 6 is a template for creating this instrument. I have provided a format with an introduction and directions as well as possible question construction and demographics.

In order to complete this tool, start by making sure the directions are appropriate. I created directions that describe the purpose of the research and allow respondents to provide their assent. This is followed by templates for different types of questions with ordered and unordered response categories. Use these templates to construct your questions and indices. Make sure to start with questions that build early interest in the survey and to place questions in a logical order. Use questions from other sources here as well. Lastly, choose among the demographic questions to include in your survey. Keep only those you find valuable. I have included basic demographic questions and templates for their standard use, but if there are other specific demographics you might find useful feel free to add them. Recall that the point of demographics is to better understand your respondents and to break down the answers to survey questions by population group. Be aware that I have created a very basic template for

Tool 6. Survey Template

Thank you for taking the time to complete this survey. The purpose of this research is to learn more about [paraphrase research question]. Your participation in this survey is voluntary and confidential. Do not write your name anywhere on this survey. There are no right or wrong answers. Please answer each question by marking the space that best represents you and your attitudes, beliefs, feelings, or behaviors.

[Remember to start with the most engaging questions to build interest and end with demographic questions]

1. Write questions with only two ordered response categories like this?

    _____ yes

    _____ no

2. Write questions with ordered response categories that provide a scale like this?

    _____ strongly agree

    _____ agree

    _____ neither agree nor disagree

    _____ disagree

    _____ strongly disagree

3. Write questions with unordered response categories like this?

    _____ category 1

    _____ category 2

    _____ category 3

    _____ category 4

[Possible demographic questions]

4. How old are you? _____
5. Are you: male? _____ or female? _____
6. What grade are you in? _____
7. What race do you consider yourself to be?

    _____ White

    _____ Black or African American

_____ Native American or Alaska Native

_____ Asian

_____ Pacific Islander

8. What is your ethnicity?

_____ Hispanic or Latino/a

_____ Not Hispanic or Latino/a

9. What is the language you most often use at home?

_____ English

_____ Spanish

_____ another language

10. What is your employment status?

_____ full-time employed

_____ part-time employed

_____ student

_____ retired

_____ not employed at all

11. In which of the following income ranges does your household's income fall? (Please indicate the category that best describes your household income before taxes in the past year)

_____ less than $10,000

_____ $10,000 to $24,999

_____ $25,000 to $49,999

_____ $50,000 to $74,999

_____ $75,000 to $99,999

_____ $100,000 to $149,999

_____ $150,000 or more

12. What is the highest level of education you have completed?

_____ less than high school

_____ high school/GED

_____ some college

_____ 2-year college degree

_____ 4-year college degree

_____ master's degree

_____ doctoral degree

_____ professional degree (MD, JD, etc.)

13. What is your current marital status?

_____ single never married

_____ married

_____ separated

_____ divorced

_____ widowed

---

you to play with. You are welcome to make your survey look different. Use boxes instead of lines for respondents to mark. Put the questions into two columns instead of one. Or choose a more interesting font. Just remember that the survey should remain easy to read and the questions easy to answer.

Once you feel like the survey is complete, two other steps might prove useful. First, give the survey to a couple of friends or colleagues to read and provide input. Besides grammar and spelling, they should check to ensure the survey makes logical sense and the questions are easily understood and answered.

Second, pilot test the survey with a small group of individuals (maybe five to ten) from your target population. Just allow them to complete the survey. You are trying to learn how long the survey takes to complete, if any of the questions or answer categories are confusing, and if the survey becomes illogical at any point. You may look to see if answers are distributed across response categories or if respondents are skipping specific questions. Large-scale survey research centers might pilot test a survey with 100 to 200 respondents and run statistical analysis on everything from item non-response rate to reliability. Unless you are working with a survey research center and possess plenty of resources, this type of pilot testing is beyond the scope of your needs assessment. But it is a good idea to learn as much as you can about the efficacy of the survey prior to full implementation. Every community survey gets better after its first use on the target population. The point of the pilot test is to assess the survey, not to gather data from five to ten individuals who are not part of your sample. So destroy these completed surveys after you learn what you can from them.

Selecting a Sample

Now you have a wonderful survey tool, but who should respond to it and how do you find them? The group of people you try to survey is called your sample. There are three samples we will consider here: a census sample, a random sample, and a convenience sample. But before I describe these, you need to understand two terms.

The first term is *sample population*. This refers to the group of people to whom you want to generalize your results. This can be synonymous with your entire community, but not always. You may survey school-age youth in order to draw conclusions about all school-age children in town. In this example, all school-age children are your sample population. This is an important term to understand because it dictates the conclusions you can draw from your research.

The second term is *sampling frame*. This refers to the list of your sample population from which you will draw your sample. The school superintendent's office may provide for you a list of all children enrolled in kindergarten through sixth grade. A sampling frame allows you to choose one of the three sample types mentioned above and discussed below. However, a sampling frame might not always be as easy to come by as a list of enrolled school children. For example, if you want to draw conclusions about shoppers at a local discount store, it is unlikely you will find a list of these individuals anywhere.

The first type of sample is a census. When your sample population, your sampling frame, and your sample itself are all the same, you are doing a census survey. In other words, you are surveying everyone. Consider the example of a survey of local business owners. Your sample population is all business owners in town. Your sampling frame is the local chamber of commerce's list of every business owner in town. Then you survey every one of these business owners. In the end, you can confidently draw conclusions from the survey about the population of local business owners, but you cannot draw conclusions about business owners in other communities from this survey because they weren't part of your sample population, sampling frame, or survey sample.

A census sample has obvious advantages. It is easy to draw conclusions about the population of interest because you surveyed all of them, and there is no need to worry about issues like confidence intervals (covered in chapter 7) because you are not making inferences or generalizations from a small sample to a larger population. A friend of mine leads the annual survey of school-age youth in a mostly rural state. He surveys every sixth-, eighth-, tenth-, and twelfth-grade student in every school district across the state. His is a census sample of tens of thousands of youth because every child in the sample population has the opportunity to take the survey. Of course, not every child does complete the survey. Some do not want to, some do not have parental permission, and some are out sick the day of the survey. Similarly, not every business owner will complete your survey despite being part of the sampling frame provided by a chamber of commerce. Choose a census sample when you have access to the entire population of interest.

Often a census sample is not available or reasonable. Indeed, sampling frames and samples exist in order for you to avoid trying to survey everyone in your population. Imagine a national poll of potential voters in a presidential election trying to survey every American over the age of eighteen every time they wanted to find out who might become the next president of the United States. Completing millions of surveys in a day or week is not sensible or realistic, so they take a sample of potential voters and infer from the responses how everyone in America might vote. The best of these samples is called a random sample because survey respondents are chosen randomly from the sampling frame. More specifically, every individual in the sampling frame has an equal probability of being chosen for the survey. In order to draw a random sample, you need a sampling frame that includes all potential survey respondents. This might be a list of students at the local community college, the e-mail addresses of all members of your community recreation center, or an organizational phone directory. Be aware, however, that when using e-mails or telephone numbers as your sampling frame, you make the assumption that the population of interest all have e-mail addresses or telephone numbers.

Next, you need to decide how many individuals you want in your random sample. The size of your sample is dependent upon your resources and how generalizable you want your findings. When considering re-sources, decide how many people you can realistically survey. This is influenced by the type of survey you are administering (mail, phone, in person, or Internet) and by the completion rate you expect. Not everyone you ask will say yes to completing your survey. At best, you should expect a 25 to 50 percent completion rate. Assuming a 25 percent completion rate, if you want to have 100 completed surveys then you need a sample of 400 individuals. The number of completed surveys is the major factor in determining how confident you can be in your results. In other words, the more people you survey the more accurate your estimate of the atti-tudes, beliefs, behaviors, and feelings of the sample population you are generalizing about.

Many people believe this confidence is based on the proportion of the population you survey—not true. A sample of 100 people from a pop-ulation of 1,000 people has roughly the same margin of error as a sample of 100 people from a population of 100,000 people. As Welch and Comer (2006) write, "It is the absolute size of the sample rather than the ratio of sample size to population size that most affects the sampling error" (p. 181). You often see this error reported for surveys as plus or minus some number. Margin of error basically means that the researchers are confident that the number they gave you is accurate within a range of values. For example, 45 percent of Americans approve of the job the president is doing plus or minus 3 percent means the actual value falls between 42 percent and 48 percent. This error becomes smaller as your sample grows. Here are some examples of sample sizes and rough estimates of their margin of error. Sample size here refers to the number of completed surveys.

Sample size	Margin of Error
50	+/−14%
100	+/−10%
200	+/−7%
500	+/−5%
1,000	+/−3%

Notice as the sample size increases the margin of error decreases, but this has a limited return on resources. Doubling the sample from 500 to 1,000 completed surveys only improves the margin of error by plus or minus two percentage points. For these reasons, major survey research centers will survey 1,000 people or more, but this is rarely an option for social service providers. I suggest shooting for a number of completed surveys that is reasonable based upon your time and resources. Five hundred would be great but maybe not possible. At the same time, surveys of fewer than 100 people will not provide enormous confidence in your findings.

Once you have calculated how many people you want in your sample based upon the number of completed surveys needed and a possible completion rate, you are ready to randomly choose who will be surveyed. To do this, you need your sampling frame and a random number or sample generator. The easiest way to do this is with statistical software that most social service providers do not have. You can also search the Internet for websites and organizations that provide randomization (for example, http://www.random.org can help with this). You can also create a random sample using Microsoft Excel. Tool 7 provides the directions for using Excel to build this sample.

The directions in tool 7 are more complicated than much of what I have explained in this book, but a random sample provides confidence and generalizability to your survey research. Choose a random sample when you are able to list your sampling frame and surveying the entire population of interest is not reasonable or realistic.

There are times when a census sample and a random sample are not possible, but a survey remains an ideal way to gather needs assessment data. You are left with a final and more convenient method for choosing people to survey, aptly named a "convenience sample." I see this regularly in my work with communities. For instance, a maternal nutrition program passes out surveys during a healthy families event, a prevention coalition distributes surveys at a County Fair, or a university club surveys individuals as they walk through the student union. Following the above discussion, I hope you now realize that this type of sample falls short of the rigor of a census or random sample. The major result is that you cannot generalize to an entire population based upon a convenience sample. If you do use a convenience sample, then your conclusions should only refer to those people who completed the survey. While a random sample might claim that 45 percent of Americans approve of the job the president is doing, a convenience sample would claim that 38 percent of shoppers we surveyed in the local Walmart approve of the job the president is doing. This does not mean you should avoid a convenience sample, or if

Tool 7. Creating a Random Sample

You can choose a random sample using Microsoft Excel (a program that nearly all office computers possess). To do this carry out the following:

1. Open a new spreadsheet in Microsoft Excel. Place your sampling frame list in column A of the Excel spreadsheet. This could be a list of names, e-mail addresses, phone numbers, or some other identifying information. Each identifier will occupy one cell in your spreadsheet. If you have a list of 500 names, your spreadsheet should now fill up cells A1 through A500.

2. Highlight cell B1 by left clicking your mouse on that cell. Type =RAND() in the formula text box (the white space following the *fx* above the lettered columns) and hit "Enter" on your keyboard. You should now have a random number between 0 and 1 with six digits after the decimal point in cell B1. For example, the cell may contain the number 0.416424.

3. Click on cell B1 so that it is highlighted with bold black lines. Move your cursor to the bottom right corner of the cell until you see a + sign. Left click and drag with your mouse all the way down column B until every cell next to the identifiers in column A is highlighted. Let go of the left click button. Column B should now be filled with randomly generated numbers between 0 and 1. Each of these numbers is associated with an identifier in column A. If you have a list of 500 names in column A, then you should now have a list of 500 random numbers between 0 and 1 in column B.

4. This is a weird but important step because it keeps Excel from continually regenerating random numbers each time you do something with the spreadsheet. Left click on column B so the entire column of random numbers is highlighted. Right click on column B to see the menu box and then left click to copy the numbers in column B. Right click on column B again to see the menu box. This time, you should have options for pasting what you copied in column B. Left click to paste the values you have copied. Column B should look as it is with one important but subtle difference. The cells no longer contain the random number generating formula; they simply contain the randomly generated numbers.

5. Highlight both columns A and B using your mouse. Left click on the "Data" tab at the top of the spreadsheet, and then left click on the "Sort" function on the task bar above the spreadsheet. A menu box should appear. In the "Sort by" drop-down menu choose "Column B," and "Values," and "Smallest to Largest." Click OK. Your sampling frame list should now be sorted from the smallest randomly generated number to the largest randomly generated number.

6. Now you are ready to choose your random sample. Based upon potential completion rate and the number of completed surveys you need, you should have an idea of the necessary random sample size for your needs assessment. Simply choose this number of individuals from your list starting with number 1. For example, if you want a random sample of 200 individuals from a list of 500 names (now randomly sorted), merely survey individuals 1 through 200 in column A of your spreadsheet. If that sample does not provide you enough completed surveys, and resources allow, you may need to try to survey another 100 individuals. Just take the next 100 people on the list—individuals 201 to 300 in column A of your spreadsheet.

---

you use a convenience sample you can ignore statistical probabilities; rather, I want you to be aware of the limitations of this type of sample. Even with these limitations, you may find that a survey based upon a convenience sample provides a nice balance to the other qualitative and quantitative data you gather for the needs assessment. A convenience sample can also be used if you really are interested in a small group of easily accessible individuals.

Most often, researchers use convenience samples when giving surveys in person or on the Internet rather than through the mail, via e-mail, or over the telephone. These latter methods necessarily require a sampling frame list that can be randomly sampled or surveyed as a census. One creative way to turn a convenience sample into a random sample is to use a strip of the always handy duct tape. A researcher friend of mine was once doing intercept surveys in a shopping mall. She needed data generalizable to the sample population of mall shoppers and planned to spend a number of days sitting at a table with paper surveys and sharpened pencils. Rather than wait for people to come to her, she decided to intercept them as they walked by. But who should she stop? How could she randomize the thousands of individuals who walk through the mall each day? For reasons statisticians can explain, simply choosing every third or tenth individual is not random, and choosing those who look most likely to stop and complete the survey is certainly not random. So she came up with the idea of placing a strip of duct tape on the floor and simply asking each person who randomly stepped on the tape to answer her survey. This allowed her confidence not only in generalizing to those that completed the survey but also to the population of mall shoppers, based upon the assumption that everyone in the mall had an equal opportunity to step on her piece of tape. If you choose to use a convenience sample you may also attempt to randomize the sample using something similar to my friend's duct tape idea. Overall, choose a convenience sample for your survey if census and random sampling are not possible or you want to draw conclusions about a very specific group of individuals most easily reached through convenience.

Of course, sampling is an academic discipline of its own not mastered easily with a small section like this, a chapter, or even an entire book. But you now possess a basic understanding to help decide who to survey. Worksheet 9 provides a place to detail your survey sample approach.

The first row asks you to discuss your sample population. This discussion will help you better understand who you are researching and who your survey will answer questions about. The second row asks you to consider the available sampling frame and allows you to answer the question in the third row about what type of sample you will use for your survey. The fourth row provides you an opportunity to calculate the sample size of your survey. This is particularly important when using a random sample because you need to know how many individuals on the sampling frame list to randomly select. For a census sample, this last step is not always necessary because the answer to the first question in the final row is "everyone in the population." For a convenience sample, this last step can provide information to help plan the survey process. If you are surveying a random sample of individuals, then draw that sample at this time and use the space in the final row to briefly describe how you drew the sample.

Worksheet 9. Choosing a Survey Sample

Sample Population	Describe the population of your community that you would like to make generalizations about.
	Approximately how many individuals are in the population?
Sampling Frame	Do you have access to every individual in the population?
	Do you have a list of your sample population from which to draw a sample? If yes, describe this list.
	If you do not have access to everyone, and you do not have a sampling frame list, what is a convenient way to reach members of the sample population?
Type of Sample	Based upon your answers to the sampling frame questions above, what type of sample will you use for your survey (census, random, or convenience)?

Sample Size	How many completed surveys would you like to have when your survey is done?
	What percentage of those you ask to take a survey do you think will actually complete the survey (your completion rate)?
	Divide the number of completed surveys you would like by your completion rate (as a decimal) to find out how large your sample should be.
	completed surveys/completion rate as a decimal = sample size

For example
200/.25 = 800

What sample size should you plan for?

Draw Your Random Sample	If you are using a random sample, then briefly describe how you drew an appropriate random sample here.

Selecting a Survey Methodology

Now that you have a survey tool and a sample, you also need to decide how to survey your population of interest. As mentioned earlier, there are four basic ways to reach people: over the telephone, through the mail, electronically, and in person. Conduct telephone surveys if your sampling frame contains respondent telephone numbers and you require easy access to your sample. Telephone surveys have become commonly annoying in America, meaning that response rates have been going down for years. This is especially true with the popularity of cell phones, call waiting, caller identification, and other technologies. It is unlikely that you or your staff has the ability to conduct a large-scale (or even small-scale) telephone survey. If you have the resources, then your best option is to work with a survey research call center that can provide a sampling frame with both cell phones and landlines in it as well as professional callers who have been trained to conduct surveys over the telephone.

I once worked with a rural community that used the local phone book as their sampling frame and had staff spend a week on the phone reading the directions to the survey and asking each question of the individual who answered the phone. It is hard work. If you decide to conduct a telephone survey yourself, remember to remain completely unbiased and only document the answers as given by each respondent.

For your needs assessment, you are more likely to conduct your survey through the mail than over the telephone. This requires a sampling frame that includes the addresses of everyone in your sample population—a reasonable requirement. Imagine your population of interest is the faculty and staff members at a university. The university directory (usually available online) provides the department addresses of each faculty and staff member. These can simply be pasted into your Excel spreadsheet for random selection or you can mail a survey to everyone for a census sample. If you do conduct a mail survey, then you can expect a relatively low completion rate. Depending upon your resources, plan to do a couple of things to improve completions. First, when you mail out the survey you must include a self-addressed stamped envelope for its return. Without this your completion rate will be nearly zero. The goal is to lower the burden as far as possible for respondents. If they have to pay for a stamp or address their own envelope they will not take the time to complete the survey. Second, plan to send out either additional surveys or reminder cards to your sample. Reminder cards are just a simple postcard reminding potential respondents that they received a survey in the mail and that it is very important they complete it and send it back. Sometimes, and with appropriate resources, reminder cards can be sent prior to the actual mail-out survey.

While telephone and mail surveys have been done for decades, the Internet has provided researchers the ability to survey large groups of people at a relatively low cost. Different options exist for electronic surveys. The first is to simply e-mail the survey to your sample. This is just like a mail survey, but you are using a sampling frame of e-mail addresses rather than physical addresses. You can also send reminders over e-mail. Imagine the cost savings when you don't have to print surveys and reminder cards or pay for postage. E-mail survey participants can simply respond to the e-mail or click on a link that sends them to an online survey system. The most popular is "Survey Monkey" (search online for http://www.surveymonkey.com), but numerous systems exist and most universities have their own online survey tools. These systems actually help you build your survey. I suggest using my tool above to create your survey and then enter the directions and questions into an online system if you are using one.

The advantages of an online survey system are numerous. Most people are used to and comfortable with using the Internet and clicking answers using their mouse. The systems tend to help you build your survey and make it look professional and presentable. And the data is provided to you electronically—many even run basic statistics for you. However, an online survey is only as good as you make it. Online survey systems still allow you to ask poor questions and to create illogical surveys. You are also responsible for choosing your sample and providing respondents the electronic link to the survey. Often this is done via e-mail, so you are back to the sampling frame discussed above. You can also provide the link in person or put it somewhere your target population might see it.

This leads to another possibility, which is placing the survey on your website or even on public computers for use by your survey population. For instance, you might run a public health center with computers in the lobby for public use. Anyone who opens the Internet is immediately confronted with a message asking them to answer a survey. This type of use of electronic surveys is necessarily a convenience sample because not everyone who walks into the lobby has an equal probability of taking the survey.

Lastly, you may choose to conduct your survey in person. While this frequently leads to a less rigorous convenience sample, it is the type of methodology I see most often used by social service organizations doing needs assessments. In-person surveys can require fewer resources and can be completed by staff who have access to the sample population. They can also reach hard-to-find populations. I know a team of researchers who study national parks and needed to better understand the attitudes, behaviors, and feelings of people specifically using national park hiking trails. There was no way for them to randomly sample a population of trail users, so they went straight to the trails themselves and asked hikers to complete their survey. They ended up with a large sample and a high completion rate. Similarly, you may want to survey food bank users, holiday shoppers, or downtown restaurant owners. The simplest approach would be to go to the food bank, shopping centers, or downtown restaurants and pass out surveys and sharp pencils.

Now that you have considered how to implement your survey, it is time to put everything together. Worksheet 10 asks you to create a survey research plan by basically summarizing your survey tool, your survey sample, and your survey methods. Note that your survey plan may involve using multiple modes of survey research.

Once you are confident in your survey instrument and feel able to describe your survey research plan in detail, you are ready to implement the survey. After you have enough completed surveys, you are ready to enter and analyze your quantitative data as described in chapter 7.

Making Quantitative Observations

You may have chosen quantitative observation as a way to collect data because you need information in the form of unfiltered counts rather than through another instrument like a survey. When observing, you are the data collection instrument, so remain aware that your role (or the role of volunteer observers) is to document with numbers the answers to your research questions. Regardless of how you observe, much thought needs to go into the observation process. Like conducting surveys, quantitative observation must be logical and systematic. Start by answering a

Worksheet 10. Quantitative Survey Plan

Question 1a   Considering your research questions and your community, describe what you hope to learn from your survey.

Question 1b   Describe the sample population, sampling frame, and sample you plan to use for your survey.

Question 1c   Describe the methods you will use to collect completed surveys from your survey population.

number of questions and end by creating an observational protocol. What will be observed? Who will observe it? Where will they observe it? When will they observe it? The answers to these queries depend upon your needs assessment research questions. Note that, when making quantitative observations, the role of passive versus participant observer is not of much consequence. When doing qualitative observation, the end result is a story of need, but your quantitative observations will provide basic counts of things that occur—leading to a set of numbers that aid in your overall assessment of need. Regardless of participation, counts should remain accurate and objective.

This section on the collection of quantitative observation data is very similar to the section on the collection of qualitative observation data in chapter 4. However, while the methodology is comparable, qualitative observation leads to a story told in words and quantitative observation leads to descriptive numbers. If you are working through both sections, then consider how they might be completed more efficiently together.

Let us begin with the first question (what will we observe?), borrowing from the chapter 4 example of a needs assessment for a youth baseball league. The major research question is what does our community baseball program need to increase participation and foster excellence? If we chose observation as a research method it seems fairly obvious we will want to attend some of the baseball practices and games. We may also want to look more closely at the equipment and fields used for these games and practices. Now consider your needs assessment and the social issues it is concerned with. Where is the "game" being played? Where will you see people playing it? What equipment are they using? For example, you may be interested in downtown vandalism. How often is the vandalism happening? What types of things are vandalized? When is it happening? If you can answer these questions, then you can answer the question of what will be observed. Keep in mind, however, that your own safety is more important than any observational research. A researcher would never sit next to a pitcher during a baseball game counting balls and strikes. Similarly, you would never try to count the things criminals are stealing from a convenience store as they held the clerk at gunpoint.

Once you understand what to observe, you need to decide who will observe it. Science is based upon observation, and being a good quantitative observer means careful tallying. Observation can be harder than it looks because you or your volunteers are the research instrument. Think of yourself as a detective who is documenting the scene of a crime. How many things are missing? How long are the skid marks left by the getaway car? How many victims are there? What are their genders and ethnicities? More specifically, you need to find an observant volunteer who has time enough to thoroughly complete the surveillance. In the case of the youth baseball league, we may have parents on our needs assessment workgroup who already attend many practices and games and could complete the counts. You may also choose to have more than one individual observe, and later compare numbers to ensure accuracy. For example, if you decide to count the number of fans who attend games where tickets are not sold and attendance is not taken, then you would have two individuals attend a game and count the number of people in attendance. These two people would then get together after the game and come to some consensus on the number of fans.

Once you decide what to observe and who will observe it, answering the next two questions should be straightforward. Choose where and when to observe based upon the most likely place and time to see the best example of the social issue you are interested in. For the youth baseball league that might mean formal games and less formal practices, but what if a team is playing out of town against a team from another league? Or what if the program we are interested in has multiple fields to play on? Again, choose to observe at a place and time that provide the best example of what you are interested in. If your needs assessment has to do with quality day care for children, you may choose to send a couple of observers into day care centers. When do they observe? in the mornings? during nap time? after school? And how many day care centers do they visit? So, how much observation is enough observation? Observation for your needs assessment takes place in hours, not days. You may want to attend multiple events or travel to multiple locations, and you may want to observe on different days at different times. As always, make these decisions based upon answering your needs assessment research questions.

Finally, and as mentioned above, quantitative observation is best accomplished as a passive observer. It is easier to keep track of the total number of balls, strikes, walks, hits, and runs as a fan in the stands than as the shortstop. Similarly, counting the number of runners of different ages and types is much easier if you are not running the marathon alongside

Exercise 4. Practice Quantitative Observing

For this exercise, pretend you are working on a needs assessment for the local Parks and Recreation Department. The research question is, how can we make our parks more attractive for the public in order to increase the number of people who use them? Part of this research involves observing the environment and use of local parks. To complete this exercise, plan to spend exactly one hour at one local park taking notes, walking around and through the park, and sitting quietly watching people. Do this during a pleasant afternoon or evening when people are most likely to use the park. Your goal is to collect the number of people, events, or activities taking place. Remember you are the research instrument. As you sit and walk around your chosen park, count the following.

How many individuals used the park during your observation? _____

How many groups of people used the park during your observation? _____

How many groups of people played a sport during your observation? _____

How many children used the playground during your observation? _____

How many groups of people ate a picnic meal during your observation? _____

How many picnic tables are there in the park? _____

How many pieces of playground equipment are in the park? _____

them. Before you create a plan or protocol I want to provide you with a way to practice counting things. Exercise 4 asks you to observe people recreating in a local park, but this time with numbers instead of words.

How did you do? Was it harder or easier than you thought it would be? Notice that some things are much easier to count than others. The number of picnic tables rarely changes and certainly not within the hour of your observation, but the number of groups of people playing a sport or children using a playground can be difficult to track. These numbers do not only change day by day or hour by hour; they also change during the hour of your observation.

The key to accurate counts is a systematic design, and now you are ready to make some decisions and design your quantitative observation. Worksheet 11 asks you to detail the what, who, when, and where questions about your quantitative observational research.

Now that you have a plan for quantitative observations, you need to create an observational protocol. This protocol provides structure to the observation and a place to document your counts. Remember, the goal of your quantitative observation is to end with a set of numbers that contributes to answering your research questions. Tool 8 provides a template for completing your observation and tallying occurrences. Key for creating this protocol is your answer to question 1a in worksheet 11. What specifically needs to be counted? Tool 8 provides one column with multiple cells to write down the specific occurrences you are interested in and a second column for tallying or documenting counts. There are rows enough to document five specific occurrences. Of course, you should feel free to use more or fewer than the five rows. If you do feel the need to count more than five occurrences, then consider whether or not everything you are counting really provides answers to your research questions. Borrowing from the park example in exercise 4, the first column might list the number of picnic tables, number of groups playing sports, and number of children using the playground. The second column is for reporting or tallying the numbers. In some situations (like counting picnic tables) you may simply put in a number (like 9). In other situations (like counting children at a playground) you may need to sit and watch as children come and go. You would then make a check mark or tally mark each time a new child enters the playground. This allows for a quick summary count when the observation is complete.

Worksheet 11. Quantitative Observation Plan

Question 1a	Considering your research questions and your community, describe what you will observe for your needs assessment. In other words, what specifically needs to be counted?
Question 1b	Who will be conducting the observations? Will there be one individual observer or more than one?
Question 1c	Where and when will the observations take place? How long will the observations take?
Summary	Based upon your thoughtful answers above, provide the following:

What will be observed?

Who will observe it?

When will they observe it?

Where will they observe it?

How long will they observe it?

Tool 8. Quantitative Observation Protocol

Date:

Time:

Place:

Observer Name:

Specific Occurrence	Tally or Counts
1.	
2.	
3.	
4.	
5.	

Now it is time to implement your observation plan either alone or with multiple individuals. Once completed, you are ready to analyze your quantitative observations as described in chapter 7.

Using Quantitative Archives

You chose this final type of quantitative data collection because the data you need already exists, you need background information on your community, or you want to prioritize among separate problems. Remember these are numbers like the percentage of youth smoking cigarettes or the number of single-parent households. This information comes in the form of percentages, counts, rates, and more. And this can mean mountains of data. My five-step plan for you to manage it is the same as described in chapter 4 for managing qualitative archives, and it makes sense to go through this plan for both types of archives together if you choose to use both. This plan includes brainstorming, inventorying, prioritizing, grouping, and filing. Similar to a funnel, these steps will help you identify the universe of possibilities and narrow it to a reasonable and targeted amount of data. As always, your research questions drive this process.

Start with brainstorming. This term was made popular by advertising executive Alex Faickney Osborn in his 1963 book *Applied Imagination*. Osborn's method focused on a quantity of ideas while withholding criticism of these ideas and encouraging unusual and creative thoughts. Today brainstorming is commonly used in many organizations to stimulate ideas or lists in a (hopefully) safe environment. However, some research has shown group brainstorming can be less effective than individuals working alone (Stroeb, Diehl, & Abakoumkin, 1992). For this reason, I want you to begin to inventory all potential quantitative archives through a guided brainstorming process. This process includes three specific questions asked of the group and of individuals. What possible quantitative archives exist? Who else might help identify archival sources? And what criteria will be used to narrow these sources? Notice that I mentioned groups and individuals. The brainstorming process should begin with your needs assessment workgroup or a subsection of that group but move to individuals in two important ways.

First, you should offer members of the brainstorming group the opportunity to provide ideas even after the group meets. Second, the group will identify other individuals who can provide further archival data sources (hence the second question above). Worksheet 12 provides a

Worksheet 12. Brainstorming Quantitative Archives

Questions	Notes
What possible sources of quantitative data exist?	
Who else might know of other sources of quantitative archives?	
What criteria will you use to narrow the list of archives to just those that answer your research questions?	

simple protocol for brainstorming. Feel free to take notes on this work-sheet, on scratch paper, or electronically. Remember, all thoughts are valu-able and this is not the place to criticize or eliminate ideas. The end goal of this exercise is to inventory all the possible sources of archival data.

The final question begins the prioritizing process. Narrowing criteria should reflect your research questions and your need for high-quality data. For example, you may narrow based upon how old the data is, the quality of the information, or its availability.

Once you complete brainstorming within the group and individually, you have lists of potential data sources. Putting these together in a formal document or electronic spreadsheet provides an inventory of these sources. This inventorying leads naturally to the prioritizing and grouping of data. Create this list without bias because it should come close to representing the universe of possible and relevant archives. Once your inventory is com-plete, you can apply your criteria with the express goal of keeping or eliminating data sources. For example, if one criterion is to reject any data more than five years old, then you would eliminate a survey com-pleted in 2001 but keep recent financial reports. This prioritized inventory need not be huge because the data must answer your research questions, and you will ultimately end up analyzing all of it.

Working alone or with your needs assessment workgroup, place the remaining data sources into groups. This will help organize your thoughts and prepare you for later analysis. These groups will likely appear natu-rally. For example, you may have several archives sorted into youth sur-veys, crime data, and census numbers. Following prioritization, you may even end up with only a single useful archival data source. Consider the number of other types of data you are collecting overall, and find a balance with the quantitative archives you use.

You should now have a frugal list of archival data sources. This is not the same as actually having the data. The final step is to collect the data from these sources and place them into physical or electronic folders. This filing process should represent the groupings you created above, though a single grouping might require one physical and one electronic folder. Survey results, for instance, may exist electronically or in paper reports. You may find yourself eliminating data sources in this final step as you realize some things are not truly accessible. In the end, you will have a small collection of quantitative archives ready for the analysis described in chapter 7. Tool 9 below provides a place to document this process. Use it to record each step leading to your useful archives.

Again, the process for collecting quantitative archives is nearly identical to that for collecting qualitative archives. If you decide to collect both, then you should adapt the process to accomplish both together. See demonstration 4 in chapter 4 for an example that can also be applied to the process of gathering quantitative archives.

Depending upon the types of quantitative data you chose to collect in chapter 3 and then pursued in this chapter, you should have a collection of survey, observational, and archival data ready to analyze. We now turn to chapters 6 and 7 to analyze all of the data you have collected.

FURTHER READINGS

To learn more about collecting quantitative data and conducting surveys, consider reading one of the following texts.

Dillman, D. A., Smyth, J. D., & Christian, L. M. (2009) *Internet, mail, and mixed-mode surveys: The tailored design method.* Hoboken, NJ: John Wiley & Sons.

Frankfort-Nachmias, C., & Nachmias D. (2007). *Research methods in the social sciences.* New York: Worth Publishing.

Salkind, N. J. (2012). *Exploring research.* Upper Saddle River, NJ: Pearson Education.

Welch, S., & Comer, J. (2006). *Quantitative methods for public administration: Techniques and applications.* Orlando, FL: Harcourt College Publishers.

Tool 9. Quantitative Archives

Process	Notes and Lists
Inventory of possible quantitative archival data sources	
Prioritization criteria	
Prioritized inventory of quantitative archival data sources	
Groupings of quantitative archival data sources	
List of physical files	
List of electronic files	

Analyzing Qualitative Data

If you chose to collect qualitative data, by now you should possess files of data in the form of words. These files might include notes you took on your laptop computer, notebooks full of observations, a document pasted with blog posts from the Internet, handwritten answers to open-ended questions from key informants, or audio tapes of focus group discussions. In sum, you have a big heap of writing. This chapter provides specific directions for analyzing the qualitative data you collected in chapter 4 using interviews, focus groups, observations, or archives. The purpose of chapter 6 is to help you draw meaningful information and conclusions from these data, and when you are done working through the chapter you should have some idea of how your qualitative data provide discoveries and generalizations relative to your research questions.

TASK 7: ANALYZE QUALITATIVE NEEDS ASSESSMENT DATA

It may appear as though there are nearly as many ways to analyze qualitative data as there are qualitative researchers. However, Krueger (1994) warns us, "Qualitative analysis is not whatever you want it to be, but unfortunately that is a perception that is sometimes held" (p. 141). I use the word *analyze* when referring to your work with qualitative data because it is not creative writing; rather, the process is logical, systematic, and scientific. My hope is that your qualitative analysis will lead to reasoned and trustworthy answers to your research questions. In order to accomplish this, you will prepare and organize your data, reduce it to themes, and draw conclusions. I will present this in five phases. But the process of analyzing qualitative data is anything but linear, which is one thing that makes qualitative data so difficult to work with. You may learn something in a later phase that helps you better accomplish an earlier phase, or you may seize an opportunity in the beginning of your analysis to inform the end of your analysis. This leads a good friend of mine, an expert in qualitative research in educational settings, to use the prefix "re" a great deal when discussing his work—reread, refine, reanalyze.

Many authors prove useful when planning a qualitative analysis, but for me Robert K. Yin's (2011) book *Qualitative Research from Start to Finish* provides the most valuable process. Yin describes five analytic phases: compiling, disassembling, reassembling, interpreting, and concluding. Again, these phases can be worked on as steps but also continually inform each other. As you move through this chapter, feel free to think about more than one phase at a time and do not fear going back to reconsider (there is one of those "re" words) phases you might have previously thought complete. Yin (2011) tells us to "remember again that the phases can be recursive, which means that while you are in one phase you may go backward or forward at the same time—backward by returning to alter something done in an earlier phase, and forward by previewing or surfacing an idea for an upcoming phase" (p. 186).

The process starts with compiling. During this phase, you organize your literal pile of qualitative data. You put things in order, refine your notes, transcribe audio records, and create a database. During the disassembling phase, you code the data. This means you label and group similar ideas and information together in order to begin noticing major trends and similarities. During the reassembling phase, you use these labels and groupings to identify patterns and themes in your data. The major product of this phase will be a matrix to help display your results and move to the next phase. During the interpreting phase, you provide meaning to your data and essentially detail your qualitative findings. And during the concluding phase, you describe what you discovered and generalize these results to your community of interest.

Compiling Your Qualitative Data

The qualitative data you now possess are the results of interviews, focus groups, observations, or archives. Following from the tools provided in chapter 4, these data will be in the form of written notes, answers to questions, audio recordings, or various digital files. Of course, specialized computer software to manage qualitative data exists, but I assume you do not have the resources or luxury to purchase this software. Still, you can create a database with your qualitative results in applications like Microsoft Word or Excel. The process of creating a database starts by transcribing any audio files into words. The transcription procedure literally involves listening to and writing down what is said during qualitative data collection. At this point, do not try to understand, analyze, or interpret your data. Simply write or type it all down as it was said. You may also take notes about the transcription as you do this. For example, during a focus group on domestic violence a participant might say "I was upset to find out the Safe House no longer exists." She may say this nonchalantly or through tears. And when she says this others in the group might nod their heads in agreement or start crying themselves. These sorts of nonverbal cues do not necessarily show up in a transcript. You may have notes from the focus group or you may be able to hear emotion in the voices of those being transcribed. Simply be aware that notes on other qualitative information beyond words may prove useful as you move on to other phases of analysis. Once you have transcribed any recordings, type up any written notes so that all of your qualitative data is in an electronic format, and upload or scan any photographs you may have taken as part of observation so they too are in an electronic format. Now you are ready to organize the information into a database.

Worksheet 13 provides the structure for creating your database. I suggest copying this format into an application like Word or Excel and extending it to cover each of your qualitative data collection methods.

This worksheet is really a template to give you an idea of how to put your qualitative information into a single useful place. You see how it expands greatly depending upon the amount of research you have done.

The first column is for data sources—the actual data collection methods you completed in chapter 4. This may be as simple as a single interview or as complicated as multiple focus groups and observations. In the cells of this column, you should describe each single data collection effort: for instance, a key informant interview with Mayor Jones, a focus group with university staff members, observations at Washington Park, or archived meeting minutes from your board of directors. If you completed three focus groups, then you will list them in three separate cells in the

Worksheet 13. Qualitative Database

Data Source	Questions and Other Details	Transcription/ Quotes/Observations	Notes
Key informant interview with? Date, time, and place of the interview	List questions here	Exact answers here	Important notes here
Focus group with? Date, time, and place of the focus group	List questions here	Exact answers here	Important notes here
Archives from? Date and place collected	Detail archival pieces here	Specific quotes here	Important notes here
Observation of? Date, time, and place of the observation	Detail things to be observed here	Specific observations here Link to or description of digital files here	Important notes here

first column. If you completed five interviews, then you would list them in five separate cells in the first column. And if you did observations at ten different sporting events, then you would list them in ten different cells in the first column. In these cells, include the name of the data collection method, and the place, date, and time of the data collection as appropriate.

The second column is where you will record the questions from your interviews and focus groups, the details of what you planned to observe exactly, or which archives you considered. You list the questions because in the next column you will transcribe the exact answers to these questions. When it comes to archives, it is in column two that you detail those pieces that you considered. Borrowing from demonstration 4 in chapter 4, you may have listed "children's art and science projects" collected from work at the children's museum during 2012 as one archival source. In column two, you would then list the actual archives—finger paintings by preschoolers, electricity projects from an after school class offered to middle school youth, or mobiles made at an ongoing art station and hung on the museum ceiling. Similarly, in column two you might detail specific things you observed, but this is not where you discuss the results of your observations. For example, you may have spent time observing a local park over the course of a Saturday afternoon. This is detailed in a cell in column one. In the second column, you would then discuss those things and areas in the park you observed—playground, picnic tables, pond, or soccer fields.

The third column is where you write or transcribe the specific answers to each question, the specific quotes of interest from archives, and the specific observations you made. It is here too that you may link to or note any digital files (like photographs) that were gathered as part of your qualitative data collection. Digital files likely cannot be added to this database like transcriptions, but make sure you describe them and where they can be found. Think of entries in column three as the actual results of your qualitative research methods.

The final column is where you add any notes that you may have taken during data collection. These might include remarks about the process of data collection, but they may also include things you learned or ideas you had while collecting the data. Did participants in the focus group agree or disagree? Was the key informant passionate about his or her answers? Did you have an enlightening moment while you collected data? Did you see or find a piece of data that answered your research questions?

Without question, completion of this database can be an exhausting and time-consuming effort. But when you have created and completed every cell of worksheet 13, then you will have a large catalog of information that summarizes and captures your data. In this one place (albeit a potentially huge place) you have compiled all of your qualitative research. Next, you will label and group this information.

Disassembling Your Qualitative Data

In the disassembling phase, you do what qualitative researchers call coding the data. This refers to the process of identifying similarities and classifying data in order to notice major trends and ideas. For various reasons, not all qualitative researchers support coding data, but for the purpose of this needs assessment coding can be very useful. You will employ what Yin (2011) calls "open coding," where the researcher generates categories and properties of data and gives these a name with the goal of moving methodically to a higher level of understanding. Start by rereading the information in your database. Then ask yourself "what was that about?" Provide a short one- or two-word description (a code) for each observation, answer given, photograph, archive, or other set of qualitative data. This initial code will help to sort and label the information.

For example, when asked about the reasons for downtown vandalism one key informant might respond, "Our downtown has too many bars, and when young adults get drunk they leave the bars without much care for what is around them. They think it is fun to break stuff and cause problems when no one is looking, and the alcohol causes them to lose their inhibitions." This response might be coded "Bars and Alcohol." Another key informant might respond, "The police don't seem to care. I never see a police presence downtown after most of the stores close. Everyone knows if they do stuff wrong or vandalize at night, especially on the weekends, that they will not be caught." This response might be coded "Law Enforcement." A third key informant might respond, "At night the downtown is way too dark, and there is already so much vandalism and broken stuff. Nobody ever fixes things or takes pride in their property. Why should we care about yet another broken window?" This response might be coded "Dark and Broken." You may code these three responses slightly differently than I did here, but I hope you see that qualitative data can be grouped and labeled fairly simply and accurately. If you have the resources, you can employ multiple people to code the data and later compare those codes and come to some consensus.

After coding individual pieces of qualitative data you will complete a second level of coding that begins to group or categorize your initial codes. For instance, many key informants may mention how dark, dirty, and run-down the downtown has become. Your personal observations documented many burned-out street lamps, sidewalks in disrepair, peeling paint, and broken windows. Your second-level code for all this data could simply be "The Downtown Environment." The purpose of both the initial and second-level coding is to move systematically to a higher conceptual level because it is at this higher level that you will be able to ultimately answer your research questions. To accomplish this coding, add two columns to the end of your database—one for initial coding and one for secondary coding. Fill in the cells in these columns by coding the transcriptions, observations, quotes, and notes, then secondarily categorizing these initial codes. Let us consider how coding can work using an example from chapter 4.

Exercise 2 asked you to practice qualitative observing at a local park to answer the research question, how can we make our parks more attractive for the public in order to increase the number of people who use them? To practice, I sat in and walked around a park near my home for over an hour making observations without talking to people. The park is large and contains a playground, fishing pond, disc golf course, sheltered picnic area, stream, manicured grass area, and a large area of undeveloped prairie grass. Figure 2 below shows the annotated observations I made at the park in three specific areas. I put it in the basic form of the database discussed above—eliminating column one to save space and because it is described earlier.

I made my observations and recorded notes based upon the three general questions from exercise 2 and detailed in the first column. Column two contains the transcribed and cleaned up notes from my hour in the park. Column three represents my initial coding of each separate set of notes, and the final column is my attempt at secondary coding. In order to complete this secondary coding, I printed the table with its notes and

Figure 2. Observations at a Local Park

Theme Questions	Observations and Notes	Initial Coding	Secondary Coding
What is the general atmosphere or environment of the park? And what kinds of recreational opportunities does the park provide?	The park is lovely with developed and undeveloped sections. I can see both the edge of town and the nearby mountain range.	Views and beauty	Overall atmosphere
	There are lots of trees in the developed portion but not in the undeveloped portion. This makes the prairie area much windier and a little colder than the developed area.	Wind and cold	Overall atmosphere
	The prairie area also has very uneven ground. I twisted my ankle slightly a couple of times while walking. And there are numerous ground squirrel holes.	Prairie grass area	Developed versus undeveloped areas
	The fishing pond and stream can be heard from all over the park, and the vegetation around them is different than anywhere else in the park. I saw a snake, rabbits, and many insects near the stream. The pond has so many fish that I could see them while I walked around it.	Water and animals	Overall atmosphere
	There is a playground, lots of benches, open grassy areas, a disc golf course, walking paths, and a sheltered picnic area with barbeque pits.	Activities	Using the park
	In general, the park seems very peaceful.	Peaceful	Overall atmosphere

Theme Questions	Observations and Notes	Initial Coding	Secondary Coding
What kinds of people visit the park? What kinds of activities are they participating in? And how long do people tend to visit the park?	Several groups of adults used the disc golf course. These were mostly young men, but there were a couple of older men and one woman playing disc golf.	Disc golf	Using the park
	Two families with very young children were fishing.	Fishing	Using the park
	I saw a couple of individuals walking their dogs, and several individuals jogged through or by the park.	Jogging and walking	Using the park
	One large group was using the single sheltered picnic table area, but other families seemed to show up looking for picnic tables and ended up eating on the grass or leaving without eating.	Picnicking	Deficient conditions

Using the park |
	Two small children played on the playground while their mother watched.	Playground	Using the park
	Three youth played catch with a football in the developed grassy area.	Grassy area	Using the park
	One family walked along and played in the stream.	Stream	Developed versus undeveloped areas
	Individuals who were using the sheltered picnic area or who played disc golf stayed in the park the longest. Those on walks or who jogged through stayed the shortest.	Long and short stays	Using the park

Figure 2. (continued)

Theme Questions	Observations and Notes	Initial Coding	Secondary Coding
	Other than a couple of dogs, the undeveloped prairie area was not used by anyone. It is the largest area in the park.	Prairie area	Developed versus undeveloped areas
What parts of the park are most and least often used? Where do people congregate? And where do people avoid going?	The sheltered picnic area, fishing pond, and disc golf course were the most used.	Most used	Using the park
	Because disc golf players moved rapidly through the park and did not gather in one place, most congregating took place around the one sheltered picnic area.	Picnic congregating	Using the park
	Most people also gathered for activity in the developed grassy area.	Grassy area	Developed versus undeveloped areas
	People generally avoided the undeveloped prairie grass area.	Prairie area	Developed versus undeveloped areas
	People did not gather at the pond unless they were actively fishing. There are really no picnic areas, few trees, and only a couple of benches around the pond.	Pond and fishing	Using the park
	Joggers and walkers avoided the prepared dirt trail to create their own softer trail next to it or across undeveloped areas.	Trails	Deficient conditions

initial codes to better play with the more general ideas that came from the initial coding. This involved not only trying to group initial codes together but also a rereading of my notes. This led me to four distinct categories of data including: the overall atmosphere of the park, the developed versus undeveloped areas of the park, how people use the park, and any deficient conditions within the park. Sometimes notes fit into more than one category. For instance, notes on people using the sheltered picnic area and other families eating on the grass or leaving the park without eating have secondary codes of "deficient conditions" and "using the park." This example may appear simple compared to your qualitative database, but I hope it provides a sense of how to move from observation and notes to codes, labels, and themes.

Reassembling Your Qualitative Data

Now that you have disassembled your qualitative data in order to code and group it, you are ready to look for broader patterns and themes. This process is called reassembling and will result in a matrix that displays your data and major findings. Creswell (2007) reminds us that not all the information we gather through qualitative research is valuable and some can be discarded. You would not actually discard, delete, or throw out the data, but in this phase you begin prioritizing or limiting the data that is important to present as evidence of emerging themes. This is also the phase I find most fun. "The reassembling process can involve 'playing with the data,' which means considering them under different arrangements and themes and then altering and re-altering the arrangements and themes until something emerges that seems satisfactory to you" (Yin, 2011, p. 191). Like any game or sport, this involves your own intuition—an intuition based upon your experiences interviewing, conversing, observing, and reading. The matrix I want you to create here is a simple set of rows and columns, where the rows represent one dimension and the columns another. But, of course, you already have a database like this. The difference is that your database simply documents your data collection methods, the resulting information, and codes. Your new matrix will be based upon major themes and groupings, and it will not contain every piece of information in the database. You may also want to create more than one matrix. In figure 2, I coded qualitative data for observations at a city park. In practice, I would likely complete observations in more than one park. This could lead to a matrix for each park, or to a matrix where the parks themselves represent one dimension. Many other dimensions might exist for creating your matrix. These include chronology, roles of respondents, secondary codes created during the disassembling phase, settings, events, relationships, or groups of people in need (Miles, Huberman, & Saldana, 2014).

Your next chore is to play with and regroup the coded data in your database. First, decide what is easily discarded. In figure 2, I would likely disregard many of the items coded as "overall atmosphere." Not much can be learned or done about the weather in Wyoming, or if I can see mountains from the park. On the other hand, items coded as "deficient conditions" seem to provide valuable information for answering my research question.

Second, begin grouping and regrouping those items you are keeping. Start by considering the codes as well as other issues that emerge as you play with the data.

Third, define the dimensions for displaying the data. It could be parks by activities, food needs by demographic groups, or crime themes by time of year. Only by playing with the database can you better understand and then create dimensions.

Fourth, build your column and row matrix. For me, this is most possible and fun when I sit on the floor with a printout of the database and a pair of scissors. With today's technology, you can simulate that situation on your computer. However, I encourage you to spend at least a little time on the floor because it generally makes a job more enjoyable, with the benefit of confusing your coworkers. Cut and paste items until you are comfortable and confident with the array you have created. Finally, transfer this array into neat electronic matrices that are ready for interpretation.

Interpreting Your Qualitative Results

During the interpreting phase you will give meaning to your matrices by asking and answering the question, what did we learn? Yin (2011) tells us, "Data do not 'speak for themselves'" (p. 207). The quality of your interpretation is crucial to the rigor and value of your needs assessment. Therefore, the interpretation will consist of two separate components: describing, and explaining the data. Description as a mode of interpretation refers to telling the story inherent in your data. What happened? Where did it happen? Who was involved? What did you witness? How did people feel? What themes emerged? Remember stories have a beginning, middle, and end. Can you find a beginning, middle, and end in your matrices? Not all qualitative data collection methods yield to description equally. Reading the journals of Lewis and Clark or analyzing the minutes from agency staff meetings might lead to real stories over time, but interviews with families about their financial worries might be harder to turn into a story. Your description may be long or short, but remember the story should capture what you learned. Also, use quotes and other pieces of information from your database as appropriate illustrations of your descriptive interpretation.

Once you have described the data you can begin to explain it. Explanation as a mode of interpretation answers the question, how and why did this story happen? Your analysis may describe (tell the story of) how a group of women experienced and felt about sexual harassment in the workplace. Now explain where these feelings come from. As you can imagine, descriptions and explanations of qualitative data blur together as well as complement each other.

Returning to my observations at a city park and assuming some reassembling of data, I can write both a description and explanation of what I observed (albeit short for the purposes of illustration).

Description: On a pleasant afternoon in the park, numerous families enjoyed a variety of activities. Several groups of young men moved rapidly through the park playing disc golf, while families and younger children utilized the picnic areas, playgrounds, and fishing pond. Joggers and walkers followed different trails through the park. It became immediately evident that the large undeveloped space (with rough terrain and prairie grass) was hardly ever used unless someone crossed through on a trail or saw his disc fly off in the wrong direction. People mostly used the developed areas and congregated around the sheltered picnic area. Areas with water (the stream and pond) were also popular. It appeared that some of the more popular aspects of the park were insufficient for people's needs.

Specifically, families searching for picnic areas were either forced to eat on the ground or left to look for another place to picnic. Joggers and walkers have forged their own trails next to the current trails or through completely new parts of the park, in order to accommodate their needs. They avoided the rough terrain of the current trails that are unkempt and trails that provide less convenient routes. While many groups and individuals used and enjoyed the park, some families left for lack of picnic space and other people made their own improvements upon less than ideal conditions.

Explanation: The park provides ample opportunity for recreation and many groups and individuals use it. However, the undeveloped majority of the park is rarely used because it has rough terrain and provides less shelter and opportunity for recreation. Because of its lack of shelter, it is also colder and windier than the rest of the park. The trails that go through this area are rough due to the elements and joggers and walkers tend to avoid them. They provide a less pleasant experience and can lead to twisted ankles or falls. The sheltered picnic area saw the most congregating, but also saw people turned away for lack of space. Some groups had to leave the park in search of another park or another space to picnic, while others sat on the ground even though they sought out a picnic area. Clearly, the park lacks enough sheltered picnic areas to serve everyone who wants to picnic at a table or under a shelter.

This description and explanation are not dramatically different, but the first tries to tell a story while the second tries to explain it. For example, the first documents fewer people using the undeveloped area, and the second explains why it is not used. I also tried to incorporate specifics from the data itself as well as references to its coding because the best descriptions and explanations embrace and utilize the data upon which they are based. These interpretations should definitely mention or use the themes that emerge during your analysis.

Following reassembly of your data, you need to describe and explain what you learned. Worksheet 14 provides you the opportunity to do just this. Write your story and its explanation in the appropriate spaces, making sure to embrace the data and mention any emerging themes.

Worksheet 14. Interpretation of Qualitative Data

Interpretive Mode	One- or Two-Paragraph Summary Embracing Data and Themes
Description: the story of what you learned	
Explanation: the reason for the story	

Concluding from Your Qualitative Data

By now you should know your qualitative data like a favorite comfortable old recliner—even if it is a chair you wish you could take to the dump. You have gathered it, transcribed it, put it in a database, organized it, reorganized it, and interpreted it. So what does it all mean? Or more specifically, what have you discovered and what can you say about your community? In this concluding phase, and choosing your words carefully, you will specify your discoveries and make generalizations about the needs of your community. Prior to doing this, recall worksheet 1 where you defined your community and worksheet 3 where you detailed your research questions. According to Yin (2011), this final phase "raises the findings of a study to a higher conceptual level or broader set of ideas" while capturing the broader importance of the research (p. 220). It also lays the foundation for finally answering your research questions. Again, these discoveries and generalizations should reflect and embrace the data. You may have one or two or many, and they should be written as simple statements. Here are some examples of needs assessment discoveries.

- Downtown vandalism is on the rise because the public, law enforcement, and even business owners care little about what happens downtown after stores close.
- High school girls in our town are the most likely to fear being raped.
- People want to see more packaged vegetarian food at our local food cooperative.
- The main thing missing in our public parks is sheltered picnic areas.

Generalizations often question conventional knowledge and draw conclusions about your community as a whole. Here are some examples of needs assessment generalizations.

- The problem with drinking and driving in our community is much more pronounced for tourists visiting town than for the people who live here.

- Spousal abuse happens as much with the wealthy in our state as with any other group.
- More people would use the parks in our city if we repaired trails and added new sheltered picnic areas.

Finally, you have an opportunity to draw conclusions from your qualitative research. Worksheet 15 provides a place for you to write your specific discoveries and generalizations. Complete it based upon the other four phases, but know it is a recursive process and you may need to revisit the first four phases before finalizing your conclusions.

DEMONSTRATION 5: SUCCESSFUL DRUG-FREE YOUTH GROUPS

A State Department of Health official once asked a colleague and me what made drug-free youth groups successful. This inquiry quickly turned into a qualitative study with a specific research question. What are the necessary components of sustainable and successful drug-free youth groups? Of course, success is a loaded term, and in a follow-up study my colleague proposed measures of group outcomes. For the initial study, the State Department of Health provided us the contact information for the adult coordinators of those drug-free youth groups that received funding. We identified six of these groups as the most successful. They included groups that were part of high schools, community groups not connected to a school, and a group on an Indian reservation. We collected qualitative data in three ways: interviews with adult coordinators and youth leaders, focus groups with members of the youth group, and observations of youth group activities. This provided a tremendous amount of qualitative data in the form of notes and audio files that were later transcribed and entered into qualitative data analysis software. While we used software for coding and reorganizing, the process was basically the same as described above. Most important was the identification of themes consistent among the drug-free youth groups and connected to their sustainability. We also focused upon those themes that affected youth participants in a positive way—in this case preventing future drug use. While interpreting the coded data we tried to describe what happens within youth groups and then explain why that might have a positive impact. For instance, we

Worksheet 15. Drawing Conclusions from Qualitative Research

Conclusions	Specifically Worded Statements
Discoveries	
Generalizations	

noticed that each youth group had an adult coordinator or sponsor, but in every case, the teenagers themselves ran the group. Youth made decisions about what activities to pursue or rules to implement. This youth leadership component explained a great deal about the importance of youth empowerment and teenage culture in drug prevention.

We played with our evolving themes and data until nine core elements of successful drug-free youth groups emerged. It turns out successful groups

- Are run by the youth themselves
- Are supported by a consistent, high-energy adult
- Focus on the positive
- Develop leaders
- Motivate the youth to be drug-free
- Cultivate interpersonal and social skills
- Provide a welcoming social and community environment
- Have consistent financial support
- Require a formal commitment to being drug-free

My colleague and I presented these findings at a prevention conference in California a few months after completing the research. We were surprised when, along with the usual researchers and practitioners, a local drug-free youth group showed up. This group was well known for its effort to successfully convince their city council to pass a tobacco ban on local beaches. The group had walked the length of their beaches picking up cigarette butts and putting them in garbage bags. They took these huge bags full of cigarette butts to a city council meeting asking to keep cigarettes off their beaches—an impressively convincing argument. Following our presentation many of the youth told us how our nine core elements really hit the target, confirming our interpretation and conclusions. The State Department of Health we worked with began requiring all funded drug-free youth groups and any new drug-free youth groups to implement each of the nine identified core elements.

By now, you should have drawn meaningful conclusions and generalizations from your qualitative data, and you should be pondering how this helps answer your research questions. But before you create these answers, you must also consider your quantitative data. Chapter 7 walks you through the process of analyzing the numbers you collected and drawing even more conclusions.

FURTHER READINGS

To learn more about analyzing qualitative data, consider reading one of the following texts.

Krueger, R., & Casey, M. (2009). *Focus groups: A practical guide for applied research*. Thousand Oaks, CA: Sage Publications.
Stake, R. (2010). *Qualitative research: Studying how things work*. New York: Guilford Press.
Yin, R. K. (2011). *Qualitative research from start to finish*. New York: Guilford Press.

Chapter

Analyzing Quantitative Data **7**

If you chose to collect quantitative data, by now you should possess files of data in the form of numbers, or have a pile of surveys, written counts from observations, or tables and other forms of archived statistics. In sum, you have a bunch of stuff that is or can be turned into numbers to measure need and answer your research questions. This chapter provides specific directions for analyzing the quantitative data you collected in chapter 5 using surveys, observations, or archives. The purpose of chapter 7 is to help you draw meaningful information and conclusions from these data, and when you are done working through the chapter you should have some idea of how your quantitative data provide meaning and generalizations relative to your research questions.

TASK 8: ANALYZE QUANTITATIVE NEEDS ASSESSMENT DATA

The weekend before sitting down to write this chapter, my young daughters played a board game where colored snails raced down a trail based upon the roll of a pair of dice. The colors of the six wooden snails matched the colors on the six sides of each die. The girls rolled the dice and every time a color came up, the matching snail moved one space until a winning snail passed the finish line. Maybe because it involved snails the game moved pretty slowly, but my girls played it over ten times keeping track of first through sixth place in each race with a piece of paper and colored pencils. Then they came to me and started reading the results. It sounded something like this.

In the first game, green won, pink was in second place, yellow was in third place, blue was fourth, orange was fifth, and red was in last place. In the second game, yellow won, orange was second, blue was third, pink was fourth, green was fifth, and red was in last place. In the third game. . .

This kept going until they read the results of more than ten races and asked "do you see what happened daddy?" Sadly, I was not paying as close attention to the race results as I should have, but they informed me "red lost almost every race." I secretly asked myself if it were too early to start teaching statistics to my daughters. Like you, they had lots of data but no real way to make sense of it. Statistics can do this for you.

Corty (2007) tells us statistics create order out of chaos. I prefer to think that your pile of numbers is not really chaotic; rather, it just needs to be summarized in a meaningful way. My daughters could have told me the typical placing for each snail rather than just read me their data table. Similarly, you need to turn all those survey responses or counts into something that makes sense and ultimately answers your research questions. In essence, you will reduce the data to allow a few numbers to represent the many you have collected (Healey, 2012). Of course, I cannot teach you everything about statistics in one chapter, but I hope I can walk you through a process to make you more knowledgeable and confident about your quantitative information. And it will lead to accurate interpretations of your research. I assume a working awareness of arithmetic but little familiarity with the discipline of statistics.

I have done numerous trainings and presentations for social service providers on how to use research and analyze data. They tend to be called something like, "But I Chose My College Major to Avoid Math and Science." I always make the point that it is okay to ask for help, especially if you have the resources. You may want to hire a data analyst to help you with your quantitative analysis, or you may have taken good statistics classes in college. If so, then this chapter will serve as a refresher and a map for moving forward with your needs assessment. If you do not have these resources, then this chapter will help you bring meaning to the numbers. It starts with a discussion of several important concepts, helps you enter and prepare your data, walks you through useful analyses, and provides a way for you to interpret the results. As always exercises and worksheets aid the process.

Learning Important Concepts

Before we start entering, analyzing, and interpreting your quantitative data, I want to make sure you understand some important ideas. These form a basis for your later work. Let us start with the term *raw data,* which refers to all the information you have collected but not yet processed (Utts & Heckard, 2004). Using a cooking metaphor, raw data is comparable to the raw ingredients of a recipe. On the way home from work, you stop at the market and collect chicken breasts, carrots, green beans, onions, celery, and fresh pasta. But, of course, you do not yet have dinner. These ingredients need to be cleaned, chopped, seasoned, stirred, and cooked before you have a delicious chicken noodle soup. Similarly, just because you implemented a survey, counted people at an event, or grabbed data from an online source does not mean you know the answers to your needs assessment research questions. You might have a bunch of people who said they are male and a bunch of others who said they are female; the police may have given you the number of drug-related crimes each year for the past twenty years; you might have counted different people shopping downtown. This is all raw data that needs to be processed and reduced into meaningful numbers that summarize your research (and hopefully tastes good too).

The analysis recipe starts with an understanding of what type of data you possess, contingent upon how you measured it. There are four levels of measurement. I cannot overstress how important understanding your level of measurement is because it drives what you do next. Like riding a bike, determining a level of measurement is easy once you understand how and practice, but it can be confusing or frightening initially. The four levels are nominal, ordinal, interval, and ratio. They increase in sophistication from nominal to ratio and the potential mathematical operations that accompany each also increase in sophistication (Healey, 2012). The simplest level of measurement is nominal and it refers to names that differentiate things from each other—sorting them into categories. For example, apples, oranges, bananas, and grapes are all types of fruit whose names distinguish them from one another. However, from the names we do not know that one is more or less fruity than the others.

When things can be ordered, then we have an ordinal level of measurement. For example, you could have the children in an after school program line up from tallest to shortest. This orders the youth, and it allows you to say one is definitely taller than another. Similarly, you might ask a question on a survey using a five-point scale. You know someone who marks "strongly agree" is in more agreement than someone who marks "agree" or someone who marks "disagree." In other words, you can order their responses, but you cannot say how much more someone agrees or how much taller one child is than another after they line up in order.

Knowing the distances between ordered categories provides even more information and moves us to an interval or ratio level of measurement. Treat these two as one level because they both provide categories, order, and specific distances between categories. The only difference is that the ratio level also has a real zero point. For example, a person's age in years cannot be less than zero (hence a ratio level of measurement), but today's temperature can drop below zero, especially where I live in the Rocky Mountains (hence an interval level of measurement). Using the after school program as an example, rather than lining the children up in order of height, we could actually take out our yardstick and measure them. This allows us to order them and to understand the exact distances between their heights. If Jimmy is 4 feet 8 inches tall and Susan 4 feet 3 inches tall, then we know that Jimmy is exactly 5 inches taller than Susan.

In sum, a nominal level of measurement categorizes by label, an ordinal level of measurement lines categories up in order, and the interval/ratio level provides distinct distances between quantities (Corty, 2007). Let me use an example of an Olympic competition to make this clearer. Three countries participate in a 500-meter short-track ice speed skating race. They finish with the results shown in figure 3.

Column one lists the names of each country competing in the race. When we know only the name (label or category) of the country we have a nominal level of measurement. Based upon the data in the first column, we do not know whether Canada, Mexico, or the United States is fastest or slowest. There is no way to order them with regard to the race, but

Figure 3. Results of an Olympic Speed Skating Race with Level of Measurement

Country	Medal	Time
Canada	Gold	46.9 seconds
United States	Silver	48.1 seconds
Mexico	Bronze	50.5 seconds
Level of Measurement		
Nominal	Ordinal	Interval/Ratio

once medals are awarded we can order the information. Canada's gold medal means they were faster than the United States, who won silver and who in turn was faster than Mexico, who won bronze. Column two represents an ordinal level of measurement. Finally, column three provides the exact time each country's racer finished in. Times give us an interval/ratio level of measurement because we have specific distances between each measure. Canada beat the United States by exactly 1.2 seconds and Mexico by exactly 3.6 seconds.

Level of measurement leads specifically to the calculation of measures of central tendency. Calculating central tendency is knowing the typical. In lay terms, you might consider this the "average" quantity, but it is more complicated than it appears. Your measure of central tendency depends upon the data's level of measurement, and central tendency drives many of the statistics you will use to summarize your needs assessment data. Remember, statistics allows a few numbers to represent the many. Central tendency lets one number represent all your data.

If your data is nominal, then your measure of central tendency is called the mode. The mode is the value that occurs most often (the most common value). For instance, you may have 100 colored rubber balls; 45 are red, 35 are blue, and 20 are yellow. Colors represent a nominal measure because they cannot be ordered—red, blue, and yellow are labels and no one can be more colored than the other two. They are just different colors. The mode of this set of balls is red because red balls occur most frequently.

If your data is ordinal, then your measure of central tendency is called the median. The median value represents the exact center of the distribution of data. A good way to remember this is to think about the median on a four-lane freeway. It is in the exact center of the road. To calculate the median you line up all the values (remember ordinal data can be ordered) and find the value in the exact center. If 13 students took a statistics exam and earned grades from A to F, then you could line up the grades they received like this: A, A, A, B, B, B, B, B, C, C, D, D, and F. The grade in the exact center (B) is the typical grade for these students. Note that you cannot say how much better the first student's exam score was than the ninth student's score, only that the first was two grades higher than the ninth and that it was a grade higher than typical. The student with a C scored a grade lower than typical. When there is an even number of values, the median value falls halfway between the middle two values or is represented by both middle values.

Finally, if your data is interval/ratio, then your measure of central tendency is called the mean. The mean value is the arithmetic average, calculated by summing all values and dividing by their number. If you want to know the mean number of shoppers per week during September at the food cooperative, then you would count the shoppers each of the four September weeks, add those counts together, and divide by four. This might be something like $(412 + 457 + 331 + 404) / 4 = 401$ shoppers per week.

Once you know the center of your data, you will want to consider how the values distribute themselves around what is typical. A median grade of B can happen whether all 13 students earn a B or if six earn A's, one earns a B, and six earn F's, so it is of some value to understand how grades scatter themselves. We will only consider two measures of dispersion here. The first is called the range and applies to both ordinal and interval/ratio level data. The range is the distance between the highest and lowest value. For example, you may analyze the age of clients who seek help for learning disabilities in your community. The mean age is 29, but the range of ages provides more summary information. In this case, the youngest client might be 5 and the oldest 37.

The second measure of dispersion is called standard deviation and tells us how much values differ from the mean. Standard deviation is used for interval/ratio level data because we need a mean value in order to calculate it (remember a higher level of measurement leads to more sophisticated analysis). Corty (2007) provides a straightforward interpretation of standard deviation when he writes, "It represents the average distance between scores and the mean" (p. 107). In other words, standard deviation describes how closely the data is tightly packed around the mean or widely spread away from the mean. It is calculated by taking the square root of the squared deviations of the scores around the mean divided by the total number of scores (Healey, 2012). Of course, I do not expect you to calculate this by hand. The range is easy enough to describe by looking at your values, but you cannot simply observe a standard deviation. For now, know that understanding the ideas of raw data, level of measurement, central tendency, and dispersion provides a strong foundation for analyzing your quantitative data.

Lastly, I want you to appreciate the difference between descriptive and inferential statistics. Both summarize data, but descriptive statistics consider the universe of data, while inferential statistics extrapolate results using a sample of the universe of data. This universe can be small (a classroom of children) or very large (all married adults in America). For instance, we might learn that 14 people died in motor vehicle crashes in our city during 2010. We do not use the number 14 as an estimate. This is exactly the number of people who died in motor vehicle crashes in 2010. We can describe what happened based upon the universe of events. On the other hand, we might learn that of 500 adults surveyed, 21 percent reported drinking alcohol and driving at least once in 2010. This means roughly one in five adults drove after drinking. But it is based upon a sample of adults. Not every adult in the population responded to the survey or was offered the opportunity to complete the survey. The first example shows the use of statistics to describe what happened within our entire population (descriptive statistics), while the second infers behavior based upon a sample of the entire population (inferential statistics). In short, inferential statistics rely upon probability theory.

For your needs assessment, keep things simple by using descriptive statistics whenever possible, but often it is more convenient and likely to draw inferences from a population sample. For instance, you would never survey every mother in the United States when you could easily draw conclusions from a survey of only 600 mothers. But drawing inferences from a sample leads to questions of certainty. Understanding generalizability and confidence makes inferential statistics more interesting and sophisticated. As we move forward with the analysis of your quantitative data, we will determine when you can use descriptive or inferential statistics.

Before we begin working with the data you collected, exercise 5 gives you an opportunity to make sure you understand the important concepts described in this section. Do not think of it as a test; it is more of a check of your comfort level moving forward. Try to answer each question to the best of your ability. Read the correct answers at the end of the exercise to be sure of your comprehension.

How did you do? If any of the concepts continue to confuse you, then feel free to look on the Internet or in a beginning statistics text to learn more. If you are comfortable with your basic understanding of the concepts, let us begin working with your quantitative data.

Entering Your Quantitative Needs Assessment Data

I once met with members of a rural prevention center who were thrilled to finally encounter an actual program evaluator even though, they assured me, they had been doing evaluation research for a very long time. They implemented mostly youth programming and were dedicated to evaluating their efforts. They spent a long time explaining their programs to me and describing their commitment to assessment. Maybe, they explained, I could help them move their research to the next level. "Well," I asked, "can I see some of your past evaluations?" The director said "sure," proudly pulled open a huge vertical file crammed full of paper, and explained that these were pre- and post-test surveys of youth—thousands of them. When I asked to see the results, they looked at me with perplexed faces. I probed further. What happened when they ran the data? What were the results of these evaluations? More perplexed faces stared up at me. So I asked what they did with the pre- and post-test surveys after the kids completed them. As it turned out, they put them in this vertical file drawer because entering the data posed such a huge barrier. They never reached the difficulty of analyzing and interpreting the data, but they were dedicated to evaluation research nonetheless.

The purpose of this short section is to help you move past the vertical file of paper and enter your data in a way that will allow for useful analysis. Data entry can be done in a number of ways. Survey research centers

Exercise 5. Basic Concept Quiz

For this exercise, place a check next to the correct answer or provide a short answer to each question. Read the correct answers at the end of the exercise to make sure of your comprehension.

1. Which of the following is an example of raw quantitative data (check all that apply)?

   A. ____ Attendance records for each day of an after school program.

   B. ____ The percentage of youth reporting eating vegetables each day on a school survey.

   C. ____ The number of motor vehicle crashes in your community that cause property damage each month for the past three years.

   D. ____ Responses to the question, "should the city council vote to raise water usage rates?" on a survey of homeowners.

   E. ____ Results of a local City Council election.

2. Write the level of measurement (nominal, ordinal, or interval/ratio) for each of the following pieces of data from a county school district needs assessment.

   A. The age in years of every student in middle school.

   _____

   B. The race and ethnicity of all elementary school teachers.

   _____

   C. The SAT scores of college-bound students. _____

   D. The titles of all the books in the high school library.

   _____

   E. High school students' grade level from freshman to senior.

   _____

3. Determine the correct measure of central tendency (mode, median, or mean) and provide the "typical" value for each case.

    A. Members of your track and field club entered numerous events in a local meet. At the end of the day, three members earned first place ribbons; two earned second place ribbons; seven earned third place ribbons; one earned a fourth place ribbon; and four earned fifth place ribbons.

    Measure of Central Tendency _____
    Typical Value _____

    B. Four of your members entered the javelin throw. The first threw 87 feet; the second threw 94 feet; the third threw 65 feet; and the fourth threw 74 feet.

    Measure of Central Tendency _____
    Typical Value _____

    C. Members drank 11 bottles of soft drink, 23 bottles of water, and 14 bottles of energy drink during the day.

    Measure of Central Tendency _____
    Typical Value _____

4. For question 3B above, describe the dispersion of data using the range of javelin throws by members of your club.
    Range _____

5. Do the following findings represent descriptive or inferential statistical analyses?

    A. A recent survey of over 400 parents found that 67 percent of parents in America use "time outs" as a way to discipline their children. _____

    B. The median grade among all students in American History class during the fall semester was a C. _____

    C. One hundred and twelve people showed up to race in the annual Happy Feet 5K run/walk. Thirty-five of these people were 50 years old or older. _____

D. Every full-time employee at the University received a 3 percent cost of living raise in 2012. _____

E. Based upon trend data from the past ten years, we predict underage marijuana use will increase to over 30 percent by 2015. _____

Answers

1. A (attendance records), C (number of crashes), and D (actual survey responses) represent raw data because they have not yet been processed in any way. B (percentage of youth on a survey) and E (results of an election) both represent data that has been previously processed. That does not make it less useful data, just not raw data.

2. B (race and ethnicity) and D (book titles) are measured at the nominal level because they are simply labels that cannot be ranked. E (grade levels) is measured at the ordinal level because they can be ordered but without distinct/meaningful distances between them. A (age in years) and C (SAT scores) are measured at the interval/ratio level because they do have distinct distances between each value.

3. For A the correct measure of central tendency is the median, with the typical value being third place. For B the correct measure of central tendency is the mean, with the typical value being 80 feet. For C the correct measure of central tendency is the mode, with a typical value being water.

4. The range in question 3B is 65 to 94 feet.

5. A (67 percent of parents in America) and E (predicted increase of 30 percent) represent inferential statistics, because inferences were drawn based upon a sample of data using probability theory. B (median grades), C (number of race participants), and D (raises for all employees) represent descriptive statistics because the data describes an entire population, without making generalizations about others or the future.

enter data to large telephone surveys into a computer database as questions are asked and answered. Callers sit in front of computer screens and type responses as individuals give them. These research centers may also mail out surveys to thousands of people. Typically, as paper surveys arrive, they are added to databases using expensive optical scanners that read checked boxes or shaded circles. And, of course, people can hand enter survey responses into a spreadsheet. This involves sitting at a computer and hitting numbers and arrows on a keyboard. The same is true for numbers gathered in archives or through observation.

The result is almost always the same, a two-by-two spreadsheet full of numbers that represent all of the quantitative research you have completed (imagine a table with columns and rows). This is because every piece of data you gather has two dimensions—a number and a label. These data pieces answer a simple question, the value of what? For example, the gender of an employee, the number of rapes per year, the percentage of students who receive free or reduced lunch, or the level of agreement of a survey respondent. But how is gender or a response of "strongly agree" an actual number? Simple: it is a number because you assign it a numerical value. I might respond to a survey that I am male by circling or putting a checkmark next to the "M," but it is your job to assign values to that response. Male equals 1 and female equals 2; or strongly disagree equals 1, disagree equals 2, neither agree nor disagree equals 3, agree equals 4, and strongly agree equals 5. Of course, 17 rapes is equal to 17, and 43 percent is equal to 43.

Your first step in entering data is to assign numerical values where needed. This is part of what makes the analysis quantitative. More specifically, you will assign numerical values to any nominal- or ordinal-level data you collected and use the actual values for any interval/ratio-level data you collected. Prior to entering data you must document these labels in order to better understand your analysis and interpretation.

Worksheet 16 provides a place and process for developing a coding scheme. You will want to complete a coding scheme for each set of data you collected. For example, you may have surveyed holiday shoppers at a discount store and you may have separately observed types of presents shoppers purchase at the discount store. In this case, you would create two separate coding schemes—one for the survey and one for your observations. If your quantitative data is very simple and already summarized

Worksheet 16. Quantitative Coding Scheme

	Name	Level of Measurement	Value Labels
1			
2			
3			
4			
5			
6			
7			

(5,423 memberships to the recreation center in 2012), you do not need a full coding scheme. Worksheet 16 is more useful for raw data and larger data sets. While I provide the worksheet here, feel free to create your coding scheme using spreadsheet software like Microsoft Excel.

The first column simply numbers each variable or measure. In the case of a survey, this might be questions 1, 2, 3, 4 and so on. For observations, this might refer to each category or event you observed, like presents bought at a discount store or windows broken downtown. The second column provides a place for you to name the variable. Demographics on a survey would have names like "gender" or "income." Other questions might have names like "approval of the city council" or "level of happiness." The third column asks you to define the level of measurement for each variable (nominal, ordinal, or interval/ratio). Finally, the fourth column asks you to label the possible values that accompany each variable. Completion of value labels is not necessary for an interval/ratio level measure like the number of broken windows, but value labels are extremely important for nominal- and ordinal-level measures. It is in this box where you write male = 1 and female = 2, or unhappy = 1, neither happy nor unhappy = 2, and happy = 3. Obviously, a coding scheme is mandatory for survey research because it allows you to keep track of what you are measuring in every question.

You are now ready to enter your data into a quantitative database. Remember that every piece of data has two dimensions. This is true of your database as well. Let us start with the simple example of the percentage of teenagers who report drinking alcohol in the past month on an annual school survey. Assume the State Department of Education gave us the data, and it has two dimensions—year and percentage of teenagers. Create a simple spreadsheet of this data by listing the years (2000 through 2010) in column one and corresponding percentages in column two. Already you created a ten-year trend of data. Figure 4 below illustrates how this database would look.

Let us move on to the example of a more complicated set of raw data. Imagine we mailed out a survey to every resident of a rural farming community and received 248 surveys back. The survey itself asked six questions about respondent satisfaction with city services as well as three demographic questions. In this case, we have a much larger spreadsheet. Column one would be numbered 1 through 248, meaning that each cor-

Figure 4. Sample Database for Teenage Alcohol Use by Year

	A	B
1	Year	Percentage
2	2000	34
3	2001	38
4	2002	30
5	2003	29
6	2004	26
7	2005	28
8	2006	24
9	2007	25
10	2008	25
11	2009	21
12	2010	23

responding row represents a human respondent. The cells in columns two through ten would contain the answers (expressed as numerical values) to each question for each respondent. Figure 5 illustrates how this database would look.

At first glance, figure 5 may appear to be a very confusing jumble of numbers, but look closer. Assume question seven asked a respondent's age while question eight asked for his or her gender (coding male = 1 and

Figure 5. Sample Database for a Rural Community Services Survey

Respondent	Q1	Q2	Q3	Q4	Q5	Q6	Q7	Q8	Q9
1	1	1	2	3	1	4	47	1	10
2	2	2	1	1	1	3	65	1	7
3	1	4	4	1	3	3	62	1	25
4	3	4	1	4	3	4	39	2	3
5	4	4	1	4	1	3	28	1	17
6	5	3	2	5	3	1	74	1	33
7	1	1	2	5	2	2	50	2	12

female = 2). Respondent six is a 74-year-old male, while respondent four is a 39-year-old female. Now assume questions one through six asked respondents about their level of agreement to statements about city services on a five-point scale (coding strongly disagree = 1 through strongly agree = 5). Respondent two disagreed (scored a 2) with the statement in question 1, while respondent six strongly agreed (scored a 5) with the statement. Note also that when all 248 surveys are entered into the database you can begin to create measures of central tendency. Assume question nine asked how many years a respondent lived in the community. To understand the average length that respondents lived in the community, you would simply sum the numbers under question nine and divide by 248.

But what if someone chooses not to answer a question, you missed an observation, or the Department of Education did not do a student survey during a particular year? We call this missing data, and when entering the data you could simply leave that cell blank. More accurately, you might create a value for missing data that would never appear otherwise (for example, missing data = 999) Later, during analysis, you can account for the missing data. For example, if eight respondents chose not to provide how long they had lived in the community, then when calculating mean you divide by 240 rather than 248.

You are now ready to enter your quantitative data into a database spreadsheet. Worksheet 17 provides a spot here in the workbook for data entry, but in this case, it is mostly useful as an example. Create your quantitative database using spreadsheet software like Microsoft Excel, and create one spreadsheet for each of your quantitative data collection efforts. In completing worksheet 17, I assume you will enter the data by hand sitting in front of your computer.

When entering data from archives or observations, first determine the two dimensions for each measure and refer to your coding scheme whenever necessary. Column one and row one in the spreadsheet should represent these two dimensions. Each cell then represents individual quantities that correspond to the two dimensions.

When entering data from surveys column one in the spreadsheet represents all respondents while row one represents responses to individual survey questions. What this means in a practical sense is you (or your data entry minions) will sit with a stack of surveys. The one on top is

Worksheet 17. Quantitative Databases

	A	B	C	D	E	F	G	H	I	J	K
1											
2											
3											
4											
5											
6											
7											
8											
9											
10											
11											
12											
13											
14											
15											
16											
17											
18											
19											
20											
21											
22											
23											
24											
25											

respondent one, the next on the pile is respondent two, under that respondent three, and so on. Knowing the value labels for each question, you tab from column one to column two and enter the appropriate value, tab to column three and enter the appropriate value, tab to column four and enter the appropriate value, until you reach the end of the survey. Place respondent one's survey in the done pile and move on to respondent two's survey. It helps if you actually take the time to number these surveys in order to better keep track of those that have been entered into the spreadsheet. Remember that if the respondent chose not to answer a question, then use a value like 999 to represent missing data and tab to the next cell.

In the end, you will have one or more spreadsheets full of numbers, and you are ready to prepare the data for analysis.

Preparing Your Quantitative Data for Analysis

It may be disheartening to toil further on the database at this point because you are excited to see what your numbers mean, but before analyzing data, you need to complete two final steps. First, the data must be cleaned. Data cleaning refers to correcting any potential mistakes in the data. This includes fixing typographical errors, inaccurate records, or incomplete measures. Can you imagine how incorrect the average age of survey respondents would be if you accidentally entered 137 instead of 37 into a cell of your spreadsheet? Or you may be waiting to hear from the Department of Education about a number for a year whose data is missing. This is the time to fix these problems. Start by looking through your database, coding scheme in hand, and checking the accuracy and completion of each cell. Remember that while this can be time-consuming and tedious, solid conclusions and the answers to your research questions depend upon the accuracy of your data. Make sure everything in your spreadsheet is correct before moving on to data analysis.

Second, now is the time to transform your data for analysis. This includes computing new variables or recoding old variables. Computing a new variable refers to creating indices among survey responses or simplifying certain measures. Borrowing from the example of a rural community services survey in figure 5 above, we may want to create an index score for overall satisfaction with city service. Accomplish this by adding together the response values for questions one through six and dividing by the number of questions. Create a column at the end of the spreadsheet labeled "satisfaction index" that sums the values in the cells corresponding to each question and divides the total by six. For respondent one in figure 5 this is $(1 + 1 + 2 + 3 + 1 + 4)/6 = 2$. The value of 2 then represents the average level of agreement or disagreement with the statements about city services. Yes, creating an index can move data from an ordinal to an interval/ratio level of measurement. You may also want to simplify data by moving from an interval/ratio level of measurement to an ordinal level. This is often done with age by creating categories. While each survey respondent told you how old they were in years, you may choose to create new categories with value labels like 0 to 10 years old = 1, 11 to 20 years old = 2, 21 to 30 years old = 3, and so on. Again, you would create a column at the end of the spreadsheet labeled "age groups" and compute new values.

Recoding a variable refers to transforming or creating value labels. For example, you may have originally coded male = 1 and female = 2 but want to change those codes to male = 0 and female = 1. This is the time to do that. Or you may want to reverse the order of an ordinal measure because it makes more sense to have a larger value represent more of a feeling or attitude. In this case old values like happy = 1, neither happy nor unhappy = 2, and unhappy = 3 can be recoded as unhappy = 1, neither happy nor unhappy = 2, and happy = 3. More happiness means a larger number. Of course, after cleaning your data you may see no reason to transform it in any way, and data that has already been processed (like results from a student survey from the Department of Education) cannot be transformed.

Running Statistics with Your Quantitative Data

Now that you have a complete and clean database, it is time to determine the few numbers that represent the many. Of course, it is well beyond the scope of this workbook to teach everything about the field of statistics, which often concerns itself with testing hypotheses and relationships. Rather, my goal is to help you accurately answer your research questions, and most social service needs assessments focus upon the incidence and size of problems. For example, how many children do not have enough food? Or how many acts of vandalism happen downtown? For this reason, we will spend a good deal of time calculating and understanding frequencies using both descriptive and inferential statistics, and we will spend a small amount of time understanding relationships among data. If your research questions are more complicated than this, then you likely need to enlist help from a professional data analyst. The most effective way to present the statistics you run here is in a variety of charts and graphs, but the presentation of your research results is a topic for step 3 of this workbook. For now, we will simply run and interpret the data.

Frequency Distributions
Start by creating tables called frequency distributions. These tables "summarize the distribution of a variable by reporting the number of cases contained in each category of the variable," and are "almost always the first step in any statistical analysis" (Healy, 1993, p. 29). In other words, frequency distributions condense your database by grouping results into a table. These are used primarily for nominal- and ordinal-level data because interval/ratio-level data usually have too many categories for one table. While race (a nominal measure) may have five categories, age (an interval/ratio measure) can have a hundred categories. To construct a frequency distribution, you list the categories of a variable or measure in column one and place the corresponding number of observations in column two. Often, archival data does not need a frequency distribution (think of figure 4 above describing annual teen drinking rates) because the data is already processed and frequency distributions are more useful when analyzing raw data.

Figure 6 provides the general form of a frequency distribution (Frankfort-Nachmias & Nachmias, 2007). I included five categories here, but you may have two for a frequency distribution of gender or seven for a frequency distribution of income groupings. The amount is specific to the categories within your measure, and these categories must be mutually exclusive and exhaustive (Healey, 2012). This means that each case can be counted only once and in only one category. No piece of data could fit in more than one category at the same time. I cannot earn between $35,000 and $50,000 and between $75,000 and $100,000 in the same year. So in figure 6 each person or observation is an A, B, C, D, or E as listed in column one; and the total number of A's through E's are found in

Figure 6. General Form of a
Frequency Distribution

Category	Frequency
A	Count
B	Count
C	Count
D	Count
E	Count
Total	Sum of Counts

column two. To be more specific, figure 7 fills in the frequency distribution for a survey question from the above rural survey database asking how much respondents agree or disagree with the statement "city services are efficient." Of the 248 survey respondents, 58 strongly disagreed with the statement, while 102 agreed with the statement. Now the data on this question can be analyzed in any number of ways, but before doing that, exercise 6 gives you the opportunity to practice creating frequency distributions from a small database. I hope you see how the frequency distributions in exercise 6 begin to summarize the quantitative information from the much larger database in order to answer important questions.

Figure 7. Efficiency of City Services Frequency Distribution

Category	Frequency
Strongly Disagree	58
Disagree	41
Neither Agree or Disagree	22
Agree	102
Strongly Agree	25
Total	248

Exercise 6. Practice Creating Frequency Distributions

For this exercise, imagine you implemented a short survey of local food cooperative customers. The research question is simply what alternative grocery products does our larger community need? You surveyed fifteen people (do not concern yourself with sample size or random selection at this point), and you created the following coding scheme and database using three questions from exercise 3 in chapter 5.

Food Cooperative Coding Scheme

	Name	Level of Measurement	Value Labels
1	Expanding Services	Ordinal	1 = strongly favor 2 = favor 3 = neither favor nor oppose 4 = oppose 5 = strongly oppose
2	Required Membership	Nominal	1 = yes 2 = no
3	Preferred Foodstuff	Nominal	1 = fruits and vegetables 2 = dairy 3 = bakery 4 = meat and seafood 5 = frozen 6 = packaged
4	Gender	Nominal	1 = Male 2 = Female
5	Age	Interval/ratio	Values are equal to age in years

Food Cooperative Survey Database

Respondent	Q1	Q2	Q3	Q4	Q5
1	1	1	6	1	45
2	1	1	5	1	21
3	2	2	1	2	72
4	4	1	1	1	50
5	3	1	4	2	19
6	1	1	2	2	27
7	1	2	5	2	22
8	2	1	5	2	31
9	1	1	6	1	34
10	1	1	1	2	69
11	6	1	6	2	40
12	4	1	1	1	43
13	5	1	1	1	27
14	1	1	2	2	20
15	2	2	5	1	48

First create a frequency distribution for question 2, "if the local food cooperative no longer required a membership to buy food, would you shop there for groceries?"

Category	Frequency
Total	

Now create a frequency distribution for question 3, "which one type of alternative foodstuff would you most prefer to buy at the local food cooperative?"

Category	Frequency
Total	

Now you are ready to create frequency distributions as necessary from your own databases. The first step is to realize when a frequency distribution is needed and when the data is already simplified. For your needs assessment, create frequency distributions for each nominal or ordinal measure for which you have raw data. There is no need to create a frequency distribution for data that has already been processed and analyzed (like survey results) or for data measured at the interval/ratio level. Use worksheet 18 to first decide for which measures to create frequency distributions and then generate the distributions based upon the general form. Make as many tables as necessary to summarize your important data.

While worksheet 18 provides a model for creating distributions by hand, computer spreadsheet software like Microsoft Excel will also do this for you using your database. This is usually accomplished by using a "frequency" function, identifying value labels, and selecting your column of data. Creating your frequency tables in spreadsheets is particularly useful when you have great amounts of raw data like those from a survey with a large sample size. However, the process is exactly the same as calculating frequencies by hand.

Central Tendency

Now that you have created frequency distributions for important nominal- and ordinal-level measures, you can begin analyzing the data further. Knowing that 58 people strongly disagreed while 102 agreed is nice, but how do these compare to each other and what do they represent? There are four ways to better understand and interpret all your data. The first is to create measures of central tendency. Because the frequency distributions generated in worksheet 18 only deal with nominal and ordinal data, you should start by determining the mode or median for each distribution. For example, the median response to the question displayed in figure 7 is "agree." This can be interpreted as the typical respondent agreed with the statement "city services are efficient." For interval/ratio level measures you should calculate the mean.

Percentages

However, measures of central tendency do not fully describe the data. To do this, we expand the distribution to include percentages within each

Worksheet 18. Frequency Distributions

Start by listing each measure and its data source for which you need to create a frequency distribution. I have provided ten rows, but feel free to use fewer or more based upon your quantitative data collection methods.

	Measure	Data Source
1		
2		
3		
4		
5		
6		
7		
8		
9		
10		

Create a frequency distribution for each of the measures listed above based upon the general form. Column one should list the exhaustive and mutually exclusive categories, and column two should contain the counts of observations within each category. The final row provides a place for you to total the number of counts of observations. I have provided eight possible rows, but feel free to decrease or expand this based upon the number of categories in each measure.

Category	Frequency
Total	

category. Calculate percentages by dividing the frequency of cases by the total number of cases and multiplying by 100. To know the percentage of respondents who "strongly disagree" in figure 7 we complete this simple arithmetic:

$$58 / 248 \times 100 = 23.4$$

There are many rules of rounding, but for simplicity's sake, always round to the nearest tenth in your tables. Decision makers do not want to see nor will they care about decimals beyond this. If we complete the percentage calculation for each category, then we can expand the efficiency of city services frequency distribution to look like figure 8. With percentages added, we can make a reasonable interpretation of the results. While over half (51.2 percent) of respondents agree or strongly agree that city services are efficient, nearly a quarter (23.4 percent) of respondents strongly disagree with that statement.

Figure 8. Efficiency of City Services Frequency Distribution with Percentages

Category	Frequency	Percentage
Strongly Disagree	58	23.4
Disagree	41	16.5
Neither Agree or Disagree	22	8.9
Agree	102	41.1
Strongly Agree	25	10.1
Total	248	100

Ratios

Another way to analyze your data is to calculate ratios. Ratios are particularly useful when data is simple and you are trying to make a basic point. Calculate ratios by dividing the frequency of one category by the frequency of a second or of the whole. To know the ratio of those who strongly agreed in figure 7, we complete this simple arithmetic and convert it to a fraction:

25 / 248 = 0.1 or 1/10.

A reasonable interpretation of the result is that one in ten respondents strongly agrees that city services are efficient. Similarly, if you serve 1,000 clients each year and 600 are female while 400 are male, then you serve 600 females for every 400 males. This is simplified to 6/4 or 3/2, and it means you serve 3 females for every 2 males each year. Ratios are particularly useful when simplifying nominal level data.

Rates

Finally, at a population level, it can be meaningful to calculate rates. We often see this in the reporting of crime or motor vehicle crashes. There were 12 fatalities per 100,000 people in 2012, for instance. Rates are useful when percentages or ratios become very small and when we want decision makers to relate to larger populations of people.

Calculate rates by dividing the actual number of occurrences by the number of possible occurrences and multiplying by some power of ten, in relation to some unit of time. That seems complicated, but it really is like calculating a percentage with a multiple of ten larger than 100. Make sure the multiple has meaning for your community because reporting a rate per 100,000 in a community of 1,800 is difficult to understand.

Consider this example. The hospital emergency room in your community reports treating 84 individuals for drug overdoses in 2010. United States Census data shows 41,500 people lived in the community in 2010. To know the drug overdose rate, complete this simple arithmetic:

84 / 41,500 × 10,000 = 20

The reasonable interpretation of this result is that our hospital treated 20 drug overdoses per 10,000 people in our community in 2010. If you use a percentage for this, then your result would be that the hospital treated 0.2 percent of the people in the community for drug overdoses—a number so small it will not impress decision makers much.

Why use a rate when you can just say our hospital treated 84 drug overdoses in 2010? Unlike raw numbers, rates can be compared to other time periods and to other places (the same is true for percentages). A rate like 199 per 100,000 people may show an increasing trend over time or may be much higher than comparable communities or a national rate. Keep in mind, rates are not particularly interesting, effective, or interpretable if the occurrence does not involve people. If I told you there were 9 snowstorms per 100,000 people last year, then you would likely question my intelligence. What do snowstorms have to do with the population of my community?

Interval/Ratio Level Considerations

Consider the important measures you identified as interval/ratio-level data. This data is both easier and more complicated to understand. The data is easier to understand because often it is simply a raw number without categories, though it may be accompanied by a time period like year or quarter: for instance, the number of motor vehicle crashes per year or the number of hits this season for each member of a youth baseball team. The data is more complicated to understand because more sophisticated statistics can be used. Just like with nominal- and ordinal-level data, the place to start is with the calculation of central tendency, percentages, ratios, and rates. Of course, you will calculate the mean for this data and choose among the other three as appropriate.

Think about the example of a quantitative database from a youth baseball league serving 6- to 12-year-olds for the past 10 years. We have four important measures: number of youth participants each year, age of each participant during each year, the number of hits by each participant, and the number of times each participant came up to bat (all interval/ratio-level measures). Start by calculating the mean for each measure to find the typical number of participants, age of participants, number of hits, or number of times they came up to bat during each season. These numbers can provide a wealth of information, especially when considered over time. Is participation increasing? Do players get as many hits as they used to? Then decide when a percentage, ratio, or rate is appropriate. For example, what percentage of participants are 6 years old?

Or, while mean annual participation is increasing, we may also want to know the rate of participation in our community. Calculate the rate of participation by dividing each year's frequency of participants by the total number of youth between 6 and 12 years old in our community and multiplying by a multiple of ten. This allows us to track changes in participation relative to changes in our community population. How might we use the number of hits and number of times at bat information? A player's batting average is simply their number of hits divided by the number of times they come up to bat expressed in three decimals. If I got 30 hits in 87 times at bat, then my batting average is equal to .345 (and I would say "I am hitting 345"). In reality, this is a percentage calculation that needs to be multiplied by 100. Hitting 345 means 34.5 percent of the time I come up to bat I get a hit.

Also, consider measures of dispersion. Ordinal-level measures have distinct and ordered categories and, therefore, a distinct range of values. But interval/ratio-level measures can vary widely. For each of these, identify the range (the smallest to largest value), and calculate standard deviation if you are interested in how much the data varies from the mean. A low standard deviation indicates your data are spread very close to the mean, while a high standard deviation indicates your data are spread over a larger range of values. Software like Microsoft Excel can calculate standard deviation using a variety of functions (for example, DSTDEVP calculates the standard deviation based upon the entire population in your database). To learn more about standard deviation, refer to the "Further Readings" section of this chapter or search for the many available Internet resources.

In sum, the descriptive analysis of your quantitative data moves forward from frequency distributions by calculating central tendency, percentages, ratios, or rates. Not all of these are necessary, and the art of quantitative analysis is choosing what statistics to use. Obviously use mode for nominal measures, median for ordinal measures, and mean for interval/ratio measures. For each of your frequency distributions add a third column for percentages. If your data is simple enough and ratios can make for strong interpretations, then generate ratios as well. If your data says something about your population during specific time periods and percentages would be very small, then calculate rates. If the data exists, then all of these can be done over time or compared to other communities.

Confidence Intervals

Inferential statistics can also describe the incidence and size of problems, but they do it using a sample of the population. If you did a survey to collect quantitative data, then you likely need to consider inferential statistics to help you estimate the population value from your sample. Most important is how confident you are that the sample reflects reality. The statistic to determine this is called a confidence interval. When you have an entire population's data then you can say with 100 percent confidence that the number you are using is the true value. For instance, our hospital treated 84 drug overdoses for a rate of 20 per 10,000 people. We are confident those 84 overdoses represent the entire population of overdoses treated by the hospital that year. It was not 82 or 91; it was exactly 84. But when we draw conclusions from 248 respondents to a survey about city services, we cannot be 100 percent confident their answers represent everyone who lives in the city. Confidence intervals tell us our best guess falls between a range of values. This is often thought of as a margin of error. Chapter 5 provides a discussion of margin of error when conducting surveys.

Confidence intervals apply to nominal, ordinal, and interval/ratio data when you are specifically considering the percentage of responses in any given category; for example, the percentage of males, the percentage of people who are happy, or the percentage of adults who smoke cigarettes. If you use archival survey data (surveys completed by other researchers), then confidence intervals should already have been considered. Confidence intervals are calculated by both subtracting and adding 1.96 standard errors of the mean to the sample mean (Corty, 2007). In other words, you should let a computer calculate the confidence interval for you. For example, you can use the confidence function in Microsoft Excel. To do this you will need to enter an alpha value which represents a comfortable level of confidence as well as the sample size. Social scientists typically use 95 percent (or 0.95) confidence, which leads to an alpha value of 0.05. This means we are 95 percent confident in our estimate.

Worksheet 19 is a checklist to help you decide which of the above calculations will be useful or necessary. In order to make these decisions, feel free to play with your data to see if results make intuitive sense and help answer your research questions. As always feel free to expand the worksheet as necessary.

In sum (and I know the statistics presented above are complex), you need to determine the size of need in your community by calculating an appropriate percentage, rate, or ratio for each measure. You need to determine a measure of central tendency when appropriate, and you need to calculate or report confidence intervals for survey data. If useful, you can

Worksheet 19. Quantitative Analysis Checklist

Measure	Which calculations will you use with each quantitative measure?
	Central Tendency _____ Percentages _____ Ratios _____ Rates _____ Range _____ Standard Deviation _____ Confidence Interval _____
	Central Tendency _____ Percentages _____ Ratios _____ Rates _____ Range _____ Standard Deviation _____ Confidence Interval _____
	Central Tendency _____ Percentages _____ Ratios _____ Rates _____ Range _____ Standard Deviation _____ Confidence Interval _____
	Central Tendency _____ Percentages _____ Ratios _____ Rates _____ Range _____ Standard Deviation _____ Confidence Interval _____
	Central Tendency _____ Percentages _____ Ratios _____ Rates _____ Range _____ Standard Deviation _____ Confidence Interval _____
	Central Tendency _____ Percentages _____ Ratios _____ Rates _____ Range _____ Standard Deviation _____ Confidence Interval _____

also include measures of dispersion like range or standard deviation. The goal of these statistical analyses is to understand the magnitude and frequency of need or problems in your community. Your completed analysis should deliver a few numbers representing the many you collected to provide this understanding. Happy calculating!

Finding Relationships

While knowledge of magnitude and frequency can answer most needs assessment research questions, it can also be helpful to understand the relationships between measures. For example, does violent crime happen to men or women most often? Or what high school grade is most likely to smoke marijuana? This can be done simply by comparing values—72 percent of victims of violent crime are men and 28 percent are women. Trend lines do this nicely when considering problems over time, and, when you have data from the whole population, comparing descriptive statistics is enough. However, population sample data like that from a survey requires determining if relationships really exist. Similar to confidence intervals, statistics must be run to test whether or not observed differences in the sample also exist in the population. This involves hypothesis testing and the use of chi square tests, analysis of variance, regression, and other more complicated statistical analyses. If your research questions require this type of analysis, you are comfortable with statistics, or have data analysts to help out, feel free to use them. If not, stick with statistics that allow you to answer your research questions by comparing different categories of data.

Seeking Help

Conducting improper statistical analysis can lead to very misleading results, and in turn, incorrect answers to your research questions. Do not be afraid of the current task. I have yet to meet the social service provider who cannot learn with a little practice to enter data, create frequency tables, or calculate a percentage. But quantitative analysis is the one place in this workbook where you may seek out help or even contract with a data analyst to ensure quality.

Turn first to your needs assessment workgroup. Remember in chapter 2 I described the qualities of good workgroup members as either possessing or loving data (preferably both). Chances are more than one workgroup member has the skills and experience to help analyze quantitative data. If members do not have this skill set, then perhaps organizations to which they belong have other members that can run statistics. Another option is to look for colleges and universities in your community with math and statistics departments that may be able to help. Undergraduate and graduate students in statistics often look for applied projects to work on and interesting data sets to work with. If resources permit, you may even be able to hire a statistical analysis center to work with you on the project. I once worked with a local coalition in a small rural community without access to university researchers or students of statistics. Their solution was to enlist the high school math teacher to help, and he did an excellent job. Be creative as you seek out help with your quantitative analysis, and keep sight of the goal of finding the few numbers to represent the many.

Interpreting Your Quantitative Results

During the interpreting phase you will give meaning to your analysis by asking and answering the question, what do we know now? Specifically, you need to decide what few numbers represent the many that make up your quantitative database. Which frequency distributions help describe the problems? Which percentages, ratios, or rates really stand out? What is typical? Which of all these numbers tells the story of need in your community? You can always return to the data, but following its analysis, you need to describe and explain what you learned. Worksheet 20 provides you the opportunity to do just this. There is blank space in the second row to put in the numbers or tables that best describe what you learned and a blank space in the third row to write a brief paragraph detailing what these numbers mean. Just like chapter 6 on qualitative data analysis, you are funneling the information into more precise summaries that will eventually help to answer your needs assessment research questions.

Concluding from Your Quantitative Data

I would be surprised if by now you were not very tired of playing with numbers. You have gathered them, entered them, cleaned them, analyzed them, and interpreted them. So what does it all mean and what can you say quantitatively about your community? In this concluding phase, and

Worksheet 20. Interpretation of Quantitative Data

Interpretive Mode	Summarize in numbers or tables what you learned from the quantitative data analysis, and in a brief paragraph what they mean
Description: the numbers describing what you learned	
Explanation: what these numbers mean	

choosing your words carefully, you will specify your discoveries and make generalizations about the needs of your community. Prior to doing this, recall worksheet 1, where you defined your community and worksheet 3, where you detailed your research questions. What Yin (2011) said about using the results of qualitative analysis to raise the findings of a study to a higher conceptual level and to capture the broader importance of the research is true for quantitative analysis as well. Drawing conclusions will again lay the foundation for finally answering your research questions. These discoveries and generalizations should reflect and embrace the data, but unlike your qualitative conclusions, they should contain numbers to describe what you learned. You may have only one or many, and they should be written as simple statements of fact. Keep in mind they typically describe the size and incidence of a problem or need. Here are some examples of needs assessment discoveries.

- Binge drinking among 18- to 25-year-olds has increased from 24 percent in 2000 to 30 percent in 2010.
- Acquaintances or relatives commit seven out of ten rapes in our community.
- 51.2 percent of surveyed community members believe city services are efficient.

Generalizations often question conventional knowledge and draw conclusions about your community as a whole. Here are some examples of needs assessment generalizations drawn from quantitative analysis.

- While binge drinking rates remain the same for most age groups, they have risen for young adults.
- Young single mothers use and need the local food bank more than any other category of user.
- Most adults and youth believe our schools are very safe.

Finally, you have an opportunity to draw conclusions from your quantitative research. Worksheet 21 provides a place for you to write your specific discoveries and generalizations. Complete it based upon the findings from your quantitative data analysis.

Worksheet 21. Drawing Conclusions from Quantitative Research

Conclusions	Specifically Worded Statements
Discoveries	
Generalizations	

FURTHER READINGS

Any number of sources can teach you more about analyzing quantitative data, and, of course, searching for specific topics on the Internet can be very helpful. I cite my favorite entry-level text for learning statistics for the social sciences numerous times in this chapter.

Corty, E.W. (2007). *Using and interpreting statistics: A practical text for the health, behavioral, and social sciences*. St. Louis, MO: Elsevier.

Other texts that have proven useful in my career and for teaching quantitative analysis include the following.

Frankfort-Nachmias, C., & Nachmias D. (2007). *Research methods in the social sciences*. New York: Worth Publishing.
Healey, J. F. (2012). *Statistics: A tool for social research*. Belmont, CA: Wadsworth Publishing.

FINALIZING AND USING
YOUR NEEDS ASSESSMENT

Step 3 of this workbook guides you through the process of finalizing your needs assessment research. It includes chapters on answering your needs assessment research questions, writing a technical report, and using the needs assessment. You will complete a few last tasks that finalize and make use of your research. Along the way, you will find more worksheets and tools and, hopefully, finish the project with confidence and pride.

THE LEARNING TAKEAWAYS FOR STEP 3 INCLUDE:

- How to answer your research questions
- How to write a technical report based upon your research
- How to use the needs assessment to create presentations, write grants, make decisions, and plan an evaluation

Answering Research Questions and Setting Priorities

Remember (as if you had forgotten), the point of your labor is to ultimately answer your needs assessment research questions. These answers represent the end product of your data analysis as well as pointing the way to action. This chapter helps you detail these answers, their support, and future priorities. It represents the final step of your research and the first step in presenting and using your findings. The best needs assessment research is useless if it fails to lead to decision making and action. Applied research like this should be used to improve services, and the answers you create here lay the groundwork for this use.

TASK 9: ANSWER YOUR NEEDS ASSESSMENT RESEARCH QUESTIONS

Task 3 in chapter 2 asked you to collaborate with your needs assessment workgroup to create one or more research questions, and worksheet 3 provided a place for you to document them. Throughout this workbook, I have encouraged you to refer to these questions as you decide what data to gather, collect, and analyze for the research project. Now I want you to finally answer these questions by referring to everything you have learned in the previous chapters.

Chapter 2 provided the following example research question. "What is the biggest substance abuse-related problem among youth in our county?" A good response restates the question while providing a brief and definitive answer. For example, "the biggest substance abuse-related problem among youth in our county is driving after binge drinking." However, your answer likely needs a little more detail.

> Driving after binge drinking is the biggest substance abuse-related problem among our county's youth. It is most common among eleventh and twelfth graders, and happens most often on Friday and Saturday nights.

Notice this does not provide support for the answer or any specific results; instead, the answer is based upon discoveries and generalizations. But support is important, and the second part of answering your needs assessment research questions is providing supporting statements. These refer to specific data interpretations describing what you learned in chapters 6 and 7. In the above example these might include the following.

> In our county, 29 percent of twelfth graders report driving after drinking or getting in a car with someone who has been drinking. Past month binge drinking among eleventh graders has increased from 32 percent in 2005 to 41 percent in 2012 and among twelfth graders from 35 percent in 2005 to 44 percent in 2012.

Together the answers to your research questions and support for those answers give you everything you need to create an elevator speech. If a colleague, supervisor, or friend steps on an elevator with you and asks "Whatever happened with that needs assessment you were working on?" then you should be able to deliver a quality informative answer before they step off the elevator.

> After our workgroup gathered and analyzed both qualitative and quantitative data, we discovered our county's biggest substance abuse-related problem is driving after binge drinking among our older high school students. Nearly a third of our eleventh and twelfth graders are drinking and driving or getting in a car with someone who has been drinking, and binge drinking among both groups is on the rise. This is particularly a problem on weekends because of teen parties. We are working on action steps now.

Worksheet 22 is the place to formally answer your research questions. In the first row restate your research questions as written in worksheet 3. In the second row, provide the brief and definitive answer to each question. Remember to restate the question in your answer. Base the answers you write on worksheet 15 in chapter 6 and worksheet 21 in chapter 7. Together, these two worksheets deliver the discoveries and generalizations you found in your study and need to confidently answer your research questions. In the third row, briefly detail the qualitative and quantitative findings that led to your answers. These come from worksheet 14 in chapter 6 and worksheet 20 in chapter 7, where you describe and explain your findings. These worksheets tell you what you learned, and the findings should specifically support the answers provided in row two. Finally, in the fourth row write a clear, concise, and stirring elevator speech. This should be one paragraph that summarizes your research and its findings.

Congratulations! How does it feel to have answers about the needs of your community? Among the many feelings you may be experiencing (relief, exhaustion, excitement), I hope you also feel energized to do something about the problems and needs you discovered.

TASK 10: SET PRIORITIES

Often, when your needs assessment research is really large, you have multiple research questions and having an answer to each is not specific enough to point the way to action. Imagine you live in a community facing serious problems with youth delinquency and crime. You know from archival data that youth substance use, crime, and pregnancy rates are all higher than state rates. At the same time, high school graduation rates are lower than the state average. Your community coalition (working with law enforcement, schools, and parents) completes a comprehensive needs assessment identifying the above problems as well as several needs. Focus groups and interviews with adult and youth community members prove enlightening and lead to this list of serious problems: underage drinking, youth marijuana use, teen pregnancy, teen violence, poor academic achievement, and losing football teams. The answers to your research questions mention all of these because they all seem to be such a problem relative to other communities. Your answers also identify related and missing services for youth: after school programs, curfew

Worksheet 22. Answer Your Research Questions

Restate Research Questions from Worksheet 3

Brief and Definitive Answers to Each Research Question

Support for the Answers to Each Research Question

Elevator Speech

ordinances, school resource officers, modern athletic facilities, mental health professionals, employment opportunities, and extracurricular activities. So how do you decide among these many answers when the data itself points to all of them? In other words, how do you choose among the many needs in your community when resources are limited?

In a case like this, your workgroup needs to rank the answers to your research questions. There are several ways to prioritize needs (Altschuld & Witkin, 2000). We will use a method similar to Sork's (1982) multiple-criteria approach. Sork's method funnels needs candidates (the biggest problems) through two distinct criteria: importance and feasibility. A workgroup evaluates each need candidate for its importance in terms of number of people affected by the problem, how much it addresses organizational goals, its need for immediate attention, and other issues of significance. The workgroup then evaluates each need candidate for its feasibility for making change in an organization and the population of interest, and available resources. The workgroup actually scores each need candidate on a five-point scale for the components of importance and feasibility. However, the method is limited in its focus upon organizations or individual interventions.

I prefer a similar ranking approach I created with the help of a workgroup using three specific criteria: size of the problem, seriousness of the problem, and the ability to influence the problem. Size refers to the raw number of people impacted by the problem. For example, and regardless of percentages or rates, how many people in our community are actually affected by fatal motor vehicle crashes compared to the number affected by lung cancer or violent crime? Seriousness refers to the severity of the problem. Does the problem ultimately lead to death or something possibly less severe like poor grades? Changeability refers to the potential to truly affect the problem within some specific time frame. Can we actually improve grades, decrease lung cancer rates, or prevent car crashes with the resources we have? Each is scored on a scale from zero to three, and scores are summed to make final comparisons. Figure 9 provides an explanation of each criterion and possible scores. Of course, your workgroup will have to further define issues of what makes for a small versus large number of people or what is meant by moderate severity.

Figure 9. Criteria and Scores for Prioritizing Needs

Criteria	0	1	2	3
Size	The problem impacts no one in our community	The problem impacts a small number of people in our community	The problem impacts a moderate number of people in our community	The problem impacts a large number of people in our community
Seriousness	No known severity	Mild severity	Moderate severity	Acute or life-threatening severity
Changeability	We cannot impact the problem	We can slightly impact the problem	We can moder-ately impact the problem	We can greatly impact the problem

The entire needs assessment workgroup should be involved in scoring identified needs, and they should do it with all relevant data in front of them. There are two ways to approach the scoring process. First, scores can be created through consensus. The workgroup can sit together in a room or around a table and discuss the size, seriousness, and ability to change each problem. The benefit to this approach is in the discussion itself, which can both enlighten workgroup members and build commitment to final decisions. The drawback is the possibility of groupthink that can lead to decisions based upon minimum conflict and without considering alternative ideas or viewpoints (Janis, 1982). Also, consensus scoring can provide the opportunity for one forceful member of the workgroup to hijack the process. After all, squeaky wheels do get more grease.

Second, scores can be created individually. You can give each member of the workgroup an opportunity to score each problem on size, seriousness, and ability to change privately, and then bring individual scores together for a final score. The benefit to this approach is avoiding politics and groupthink, but you lose any possible value that comes from discussing the scoring within the group. Of course, you could combine these two approaches by having group members score each problem individually and come together to create consensus scores.

Regardless of how you score the three criteria, create a final score for each problem with a simple arithmetic equation.

Final Problem Score = Size + Seriousness + Changeability

Scores will range from a possible low of 0 to a possible high of 9. Then you can rank them to set priorities among identified needs. Let us revisit the above example of a community facing numerous problems among its youth including underage drinking, youth marijuana use, teen pregnancy, teen violence, poor academic achievement, and losing football teams. The needs assessment workgroup might come together and consensus score each of these as shown in figure 10.

Notice that, while the workgroup should create these scores with your needs assessment data in front of them, there is an inevitable subjectivity to the scoring process. Why, for example, might the group think youth drinking can be changed more easily than youth marijuana use? Or why might the group see teen pregnancy or poor grades as more seri-

Figure 10. Example Scores and Prioritization of Needs for Youth

Identified Problem	Size	Seriousness	Changeability	Total
Poor academic achievement	3	3	2	8
Underage drinking	2	2	3	7
Youth marijuana use	2	2	2	6
Teen pregnancy	1	3	2	6
Losing football teams	1	1	2	4

ous than losing a football game? Always base justifications for decisions upon data, but ultimately data needs to be interpreted. Your needs assessment workgroup must construe meaning for itself.

Use this prioritization process when your needs assessment research leads to more answers than your resources can possible deal with and you need to narrow your targeted problems. If your answers are simple and straightforward, you likely do not need a prioritization process and can skip this step and move straight to chapter 9.

Demonstration 6: Wyoming's Comprehensive Statewide Needs Assessment

The preface to this workbook mentioned a statewide needs assessment I completed with a State Epidemiological Workgroup to determine Wyoming's biggest substance abuse-related need. Our research question was quite simple: which substance abuse-related problems should our project target? However, more identified needs rose to the surface than resources from this one project could effectively address. Should we focus upon mothers who smoke during pregnancy or drunk drivers? Should we target methamphetamine use or suicide (which can often be related to substance abuse)? Using only state-level archival measures, the group collected every possible piece of data related to substance use and filtered them first by considering the quantitative measures in a number of ways. We looked at our national ranking, actual values, trends over time, and the number of individuals in Wyoming affected by the problem.

A couple of things became clear when first attempting to answer the research question. First, there are two types of substance-related problems—consumption and consequences. Consumption refers to the actual use of alcohol, tobacco, and other drugs, while consequences refer to those bad things that happen when they are used (lung cancer, crime, drunk driving).

Second, 25 separate indicators really stood out beyond all others as the biggest problems (14 consumption indicators and 11 consequence indicators). The group knew this was far too many to consider doing something about, and we needed to prioritize them further. So we met to score each on size, seriousness, and changeability. For consequences, scores ranged from a high of 8 for alcohol dependence or abuse to a low of 3 for chronic liver disease. For consumption, scores ranged from a high of 8 for youth smoking and drinking and adult binge drinking to a low of 4 for youth smokeless tobacco use. In the end, the workgroup prioritized four consumption areas (binge drinking, underage drinking, youth cigarette smoking, and smoking among pregnant women) and four consequence areas (suicide, alcohol dependence and abuse, alcohol-related motor vehicle crashes, and alcohol-related crime).

This was still too many problems to address with one project, but the workgroup recognized Wyoming's major substance abuse-related consequences were primarily driven by alcohol use. Their prioritization led to two specific answers to the original research question, which in turn pointed the way to action. These answers were:

- The primary target for prevention efforts should be underage drinking and adult binge drinking. Underage drinking refers to any use of alcohol by anyone under the age of 21, while adult binge drinking refers to those 18 years and older who have five or more drinks on any one occasion.
- The secondary target for prevention efforts should be the most significant consequences of the misuse of alcohol in Wyoming: alcohol dependence and abuse, alcohol-related motor vehicle crashes, and alcohol-related crime.

At this point in the workbook, you have answered specific research questions with solid research and sound logic. You are now ready to document your research and put your answers to good use.

FURTHER READINGS

To learn more about writing and answering research questions, consult a good book on social science research or writing research papers. Here are a couple of my favorites.

Creswell, J. W. (2009). *Research design: Qualitative, quantitative, and mixed methods approaches*. Thousand Oaks, CA: Sage Publications.

Meyer, M. (1994). *The little, brown guide to writing research papers.* New York: Harper Collins College Publishers.

To learn more about the prioritization of needs consider the following text.

Altschuld, J. W., & Witkin, B. R. (2000). *From needs assessment to action: Transforming needs into solution strategies.* Thousand Oaks, CA: Sage Publications.

Writing the Technical Report

Whether you believe it or not, by completing chapters 1 through 8 of this workbook, you have become a scientist. You may still not fully grasp Einstein's general and specific theories of relativity, but you successfully engaged in the scientific process. And you moved from thinking "I pretty much already know what the problems and needs in my community are" to "my sound research has given me a robust understanding of my community's problems and needs." As a scientist, you must document your work in a way that details your efforts, findings, and conclusions. Generally, this means another scientist could pick up the documentation and replicate the study. Of course, we are still dealing with a social service needs assessment and not a publication in the *Astrophysical Journal*, so do not put too much pressure on yourself.

Needs assessment documentation most often comes in the form of a technical report, and the report serves as the foundation for use of your needs assessment in future decision making, grant writing, and presentations. In reality, even fewer people will read the entire technical report than read the *Astrophysical Journal*. Community leaders might read the executive summary; staff may skim through it; decision makers will skip to the findings section; your family will leave it unopened on the kitchen counter (that is what my family does anyway). The report is important, nonetheless, because it confirms the scientific process and provides historical documentation for future research. Imagine how much more simple this workbook would be if someone had documented something similar five or ten years earlier.

TASK 11: WRITE YOUR TECHNICAL NEEDS ASSESSMENT REPORT

This chapter describes in detail the process of writing the technical report and gives you a tool for making it happen. And (good news) you have already done much of the work. I created the worksheets and tools in this book to inform sections of your final technical report. For instance, worksheet 3 provides some of what you need in the introduction, and you can simply rewrite worksheet 9 in your methods section if needed. The technical report contains nine sections. I describe each in detail below. These sections include: title pages, a description of the needs assessment workgroup, an executive summary, an introduction, methods, findings, conclusions, references, and appendixes. Tool 10 provides a template for the technical report where each section refers to the appropriate worksheets and information needed to complete a quality document. Feel free to personalize this document to reflect your own organization.

Most technical reports are written in third-person singular or plural to appear objective and scientific. In other words, use he, she, or one rather than I, we, or you. Generally, scientific publications avoid pronouns altogether. Instead of writing "I spent three hours observing families at the park," write "researchers observed families at the park for three hours" or "families at the park were observed for three hours." More recently (and depending upon the audience), applied researchers have written technical reports referring to themselves as "we," but you should decide what writing style is best suited for your report and audience.

Pearsall and Cook (2010) teach writers about seven excellent principles for technical writing. These include knowing your purpose and writing situation, knowing your audience and their situation, choosing and organizing your content around the purpose and audience, writing clearly and precisely, using good page design, thinking visually, and writing ethically. I hope you already understand most of these, and I encourage you to look into any of the principles further if you have questions. Overall, keep a couple of things in mind.

Know why you are writing and for whom you are writing. By now your purpose should be clear—you are completing a community needs assessment in order to answer specific research questions. Your audience might be less obvious. When I write, I try to think of one or two individuals who typify my target audience. That may be a project director, an agency

Tool 10. The Technical Report

Report Title
Report Subtitle
[The title and subtitle should reflect your
research questions and community]

Organization
Publishing Date
[Month and Year]

Report title
Report subtitle

By

Author, Title
Author, Title
Author, Title

Organization
Address
E-mail and website
Phone and fax numbers

In collaboration with:
Organization
Contact person
Address
E-mail and website
Phone and fax numbers

Under contract to:
Organization
Contact person
Address
E-mail and website
Phone and fax numbers

Citation for this document: Organization. (Year). Report Title: Report Subtitle, by first author's last name and initials, second author's last name and initials, third author's last name and initials. City, State: Publishing Organization.
© Publishing Organization, Year.

Table of Contents

1. Needs Assessment Workgroup ....
2. Executive Summary ....
3. Introduction...
4. Methods ....
5. Findings ....
6. Conclusions ....
7. References...
8. Appendix A...
9. Appendix B...

List of Tables

1. Table 1: Title ....
2. Table 2: Title ....
3. Table 3: Title ....

List of Figures

1. Figure 1: Title ....
2. Figure 2: Title ....
3. Figure 3: Title ....

Needs Assessment Workgroup

[In this section document the members of your needs assessment workgroup, their organizations and titles, and their contribution if appropriate. Refer to Worksheet 2 to write this section.]

Executive Summary

[Summarize the methods, findings, and conclusions of the technical report here in a way that lengthens your elevator speech. This should be the last section of the report you craft. Refer to Worksheet 22 and the completed technical report to write this section.]

Introduction

[Present the topic of your research, provide background, state your research questions, describe your community, and let the reader know about the organization of the technical report. Refer to Worksheets 1 and 3 to write this section.]

Methods
[Describe your research in a way that can be replicated by other researchers. Describe how you collected and how you analyzed your qualitative and quantitative data. Refer to Chapters 4, 5, 6, and 7 and to Worksheets 5, 6, 7, 9, 10, 11, 13, 18, and 19 as appropriate to write this section.]

Findings
[Describe your findings and results in this section, using mostly tables and figures. Use text for opening and closing paragraphs and to briefly describe each finding. Limit this section to findings that are relevant to your research questions, interesting to the reader, and lead directly to your conclusions. Do not provide a discussion of what you learned or specific answers to your research questions. Refer to Chapters 6 and 7 and to Worksheets 13, 14, 18, 19, and 20 to write this section.]

Conclusions
[Discuss your discoveries and generalizations and provide specific answers to your research questions in this section. You may also choose to provide further discussion of the meaning and implications of your needs assessment findings. Refer to Worksheets 15, 21, and 22 to write this section.]

References
[List the citations for any literature or publicly available archival data in this section. Follow the accepted format in your discipline when writing citations or refer to the publication manual of the American Psychological Association to write this section.]

Appendixes
[Append research elements readers may want or need to see to better understand your needs assessment but that do not belong in other sections. This includes data collection instruments and protocols as well as more complex data analysis. Label each set of materials as Appendix A, Appendix B, Appendix C, and so on. Refer to Chapters 4 through 7 on the collection and analysis of data to identify appropriate items and create this section.]

head, or a city council member. As I write this book I imagine my wife—a social service provider herself—reading it. Write plainly and exactly. One goal of science is to enlighten and elucidate. You should have nothing to hide and hide nothing. This will also ensure integrity in your writing. I also hope you have at least a little fun and find some pride in the finished product.

Title Pages

Three title pages exist to tell readers the what and when of research as well as giving them a table of contents. The cover page of your report should contain a full title and subtitle if you desire. The title should be general, descriptive, potentially catchy, and in a larger font than the rest of the document, and it should probably contain the words "needs assessment." A good place to start when thinking of a title is with your research questions and definition of community. Something like "Vandalism in Lincoln, Nebraska: A Needs Assessment Study of the Magnitude and Causes of Damage in Our Downtown" works just fine. Under the title, remember to put the name of your organization and the date you officially make your report public—month and year are adequate. There is no reason to put an author's name on the cover. Lastly, add some color, a logo, and an image that reflects the research topic to the cover page to give it a more professional and engaging look.

The second title page contains the publication details. Begin by restating the title followed by the author or authors of the report and their titles. Next comes the name and contact information for your organization. If the research was completed in collaboration or under contract to other organizations, then include those details here as well. Often my work is under contract to another agency—the State Department of Transportation, for example. I include the name of my contact there and the agency contact information. Follow this with a citation for the report. Others may want to reference your work, and it is best to provide them a common reference to use. The citation also lends an air of professionalism to the report and says to the reader that this is a serious and legitimate document. Feel free to follow the publication manual for your field when creating this citation. Tool 10 gives you one example of how technical reports are often cited. On the final line of the second title page, place your copyright using the copyright symbol, your organization, and the year of publication. Some of this may seem redundant, but it is important to cover all the bases when providing publishing information.

Reserve the third title page for a table of contents. Unlike a great novel, your technical report should not build mystery or leave anything to the imagination of the reader. From the beginning the reader should know what to expect. A table of contents does this and also provides details on where to find different sections of the report. This is important for all readers, but especially for decision makers and others who need to quickly understand your methods or findings. Word processing and publishing software have multiple ways to create a table of contents and can even link titles like "methods" or "conclusions" to page numbers in the document. Of course, you can simply keep track of this yourself. Regardless of how you create the table of contents, it should be one of the last things you check prior to publishing the report. The table of contents should at the very least include each of the sections of your report. If your analysis results in numerous charts, graphs, or tables, then you may also want to include a list of tables or a list of figures on your table of contents page. Do not number the three title pages. Page numbers will appear later in the report starting with the next section.

Workgroup

From here, each section of your report should start with a heading. In longer and more complicated reports these are numbered, but in shorter reports numbering is not always necessary. Like your title, put section headings in a larger font to help them stand apart from the text. Begin numbering pages with this first section. Keep in mind, while this is the first page with a number, it is not the first page of the report. Count every page starting with the cover page and begin numbering the workgroup section with the appropriate page number. In tool 10, this would be page 4. It is also here that you may choose to start a header containing a shortened title, the name of your organization, and the publication year.

The purpose of the workgroup section is to describe and give credit to members who contributed to the needs assessment research. Complete this section using:

- Worksheet 2

Indeed, you may simply copy the table from worksheet 2 into the section. You may also want to add a little text describing the workgroup and thanking them for their tireless efforts, but remember that your readers do not yet know what you did or what you accomplished. Do not try to provide that information here when it is best described in later sections of the report.

Executive Summary

The goal of an executive summary is to encapsulate the entire project in one or two pages for the type of people who likely do not have time to read any more than this. The executive summary is a slightly longer version of your elevator speech. Lengthen the speech by providing a short description of your methods, findings, and conclusions. This is not the place to include charts or tables or go into a detailed discussion of a survey instrument; rather, provide the basic facts. Using bullet points here to list major findings and conclusions can be very effective. Of course, this means that, while the executive summary falls at the beginning of the report, you should write it last. For now, skip it, write all other sections, and come back to your summary. Complete this section using:

- Worksheet 22
- The full technical report

Introduction

The introduction section should present the topic of your research, any necessary background, and the organization of the report. It should also clearly state your research questions and clearly define your community of interest. More specifically, open with a paragraph describing how desire for this needs assessment research arose. Was there a specific event, funding opportunity, or situation that turned people's attention to this issue? Then describe the process for getting started. Include the creation of your needs assessment workgroup and how they came together to detail your research questions and define your community. The next paragraph should specifically state these research questions. This can even be done with bullet points or italics to ensure understanding and to set the questions apart from the text. Follow this with a detailed description of your community. You may find that simple text best describes the community, or you may want to include tables to illustrate a target population. Complete this section using:

- Worksheet 1
- Worksheet 3

After introducing the topic, research questions, and community, describe what is to come. This can be very deliberate. In my technical reports, I actually write "This document contains nine sections," and then go on to list them from executive summary to appendixes.

Methods

The methods section should describe your research in a way that can be replicated by other researchers without being boring or too long. In reality, you do not want to write every detail of your methods in this section, just enough that readers appreciate what you did and how you did it. No more and no less. For instance, you do want the reader know where you observed, for how long, and how many times, but you do not need to tell them where you sat, what you ate, and the kind of pencil and paper you used for taking notes. In general, you will describe two processes: how you collected data and how you analyzed data. Actual instruments like surveys or focus group protocols are referenced here and appear later in your appendixes. This will take several paragraphs, at least one paragraph for each data collection method and one paragraph for each analysis you completed. Start by describing how you collected data using:

- Chapter 4
- Chapter 5
- Worksheets 5, 6, 7, 9, 10, and 11 where appropriate

Next describe how you analyzed data using:

- Chapter 6
- Chapter 7

- Worksheet 13
- Worksheet 18
- Worksheet 19

Findings

As the title implies, describe what you found in this section. Many scientists call this the "results" section because it is where researchers communicate the results of their work, but I prefer "findings" because it suggests you were on an exciting quest for knowledge. However, this is not the place to interpret your findings or specifically answer your research questions. That will come later in the conclusions section. For now, simply detail what you found after collecting and analyzing your qualitative and quantitative data. Lindsay (2011) reminds us findings "should be presented clearly and clinically without comment" (p. 31). But he also encourages writers to limit findings because not everything you learned can be pertinent to the study. Limit this section to results that are relevant to the research questions, interesting to the reader, and lead directly to your conclusions section.

While written text is important in the findings section, restrict it to an opening and closing paragraph and brief descriptions of each finding. Otherwise, you should present your results in tables and figures. This is particularly true for quantitative findings, but it can also be true for qualitative findings. Certainly results of a focus group or key informant interviews include quotes or written descriptions of discoveries, but these too are best communicated to the reader in separate tables or boxes that set the important information apart from your written text. Remember, this section is not the place to interpret what you learned from qualitative data collection and analysis; instead, here you simply state what you discovered. Thinking back to chapter 6, this refers to the reassembling and interpreting phases of qualitative analysis. Thinking back to chapter 7, this refers to the analysis and interpretation sections that lead specifically to the few numbers that represent the many. When detailing the results of your qualitative research use:

- Chapter 6
- Worksheet 13
- Worksheet 14

When detailing the results of your quantitative research use:

- Chapter 7
- Worksheet 18
- Worksheet 19
- Worksheet 20

Let me be more specific about the creation of tables and figures. Tables refer to any data presented in columns and rows, while figures include charts, graphs, and other illustrations. Each should be numbered and given a descriptive title that by itself tells the reader exactly what they see. When you provide a title for a table or figure imagine your reader has no other text to describe what they are looking at. Would they still understand what it means? An example of a poor title might be "Table 1: High School Grades." This can be better titled as "Table 1: Typical Math Grades for Ninth through Twelfth Graders in Polk County School District 1 for 2012." If you use archival data (like grades), then you should also include the data source under the table. For example, "Data source: Polk County School District 1 Superintendent's Office."

Like everything else in your technical report, tables should be clear and precise. Remember, they should not present all the information (qualitative or quantitative); instead, tables should summarize findings in a way that allows the reader to easily see the results of your research. Of course, tables can be very complex, but I encourage you to keep them simple and with two dimensions similar to the frequency tables you created in worksheet 18. I have presented a few tables throughout this book, and, while my format is not the only way to display tables, it works well for my own technical reports. A template for this table structure is included in figure 11.

Begin with a descriptive title. Then create a table with the correct number of rows and columns to include labels for categories and relevant data. I usually shade in and center the top row of labels to set it apart from other information. Each cell in the first row describes what is under it, and the first cell in the upper left corner actually describes categories that appear in the first column. This column is left justified while the data that appear in all other columns are right justified. Often the final

Figure 11. Template for Tables in the Technical Report

Table X: Descriptive Title

Categories	Label One	Label Two	Label Three	Label Four
Category One	Data	Data	Data	Data
Category Two	Data	Data	Data	Data
Category Three	Data	Data	Data	Data
Category Four	Data	Data	Data	Data
Total	Data	Data	Data	Data

Data Source: If from archival data

row includes totals, but it does not have to. Remember that this table is not equivalent to the databases you created in chapters 6 or 7. It should be a summary of what you learned. In the case of qualitative data, tables may be larger and contain quotes and descriptive groupings. Many of the worksheets in this book (like worksheets 7 or 14) are actually tables that contain descriptions and groupings of information. Tables can also be very simple and look more like callout boxes with titles, labels, and relevant quotes. Be creative as you generate your tables, but recall that the goal of a table is to summarize and make clear your findings.

Figures can be charts, graphs, and illustrations of any kind. These are most useful when summarizing and illustrating your quantitative data. The goal of a chart or graph is to visually represent the data in a way that makes it come alive for the reader. I can show an increase in the percent of youth smoking marijuana each year in a table, but a red trend line makes this change jump off the page. Use two key types of charts when presenting your needs assessment results. First, bar charts present quantities or frequencies among different categories. When you built your quantitative database, I told you there were two dimensions that answered a simple question: the value of what? For example, the percentage of elementary school students who receive free and reduced lunches. A bar chart can illustrate this with one dimension being the percentage from 0 to 100 and the other dimension being each grade from first through fifth.

Figure 12. Template for Bar Charts in the Technical Report

Chart X: Descriptive Title

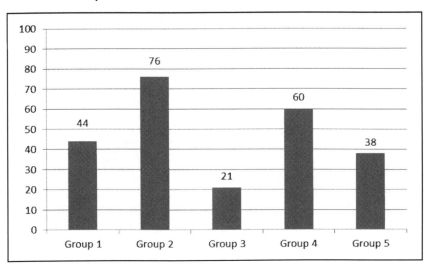

Data Source: If from archival data

This allows the reader to quickly compare the percentage of students in second grade who receive free and reduced lunches to those in fourth grade or fifth grade who receive free and reduced lunches. A template for this chart structure is included in figure 12.

Bar charts can represent raw data, percentages, rates, and ratios, but they are most useful for percentages. In general, raw data should always be summarized into percentages or rates. Ratios are most useful as basic text statements. Bar charts using percentages have the advantage of a clear scale for one dimension (0 to 100). If you decide to change this scale to make small differences more evident (0 to 25 for example), then you should alert the reader to this decision. Again, when using archival data, include the data source under the chart. I prefer bar charts to pie charts because the length of bars is much easier to compare than the size of triangles. Where I work, we joke that pie charts are only useful when presenting data on pies or pizza. However, they are also commonly used when comparing amounts of money.

Second, line graphs present quantities or frequencies among different categories where one of the dimensions usually represents time. You can present time in any number of ways depending upon your data, but most common is by year. This means your chart represents one or more trend lines and answers the question, how did the quantity or frequency change over time? Place time categories (like 2003, 2004, 2005, 2006, and 2007) on the horizontal axis of the chart and frequency (like percentage) on the vertical axis. For instance, the percentage of elementary students receiving free and reduced lunches between 2001 and 2011 would create a line that moved up and down from left to right connecting dots that represent the exact percentages of students. If we wanted this for each grade there would be five lines representing first through fifth grades that could then be compared over ten years. A template for a chart showing a trend line is included in figure 13.

I prefer two-dimensional charts to three-dimensional charts, because the more simply the data is presented, the more clear it becomes for the reader. However, feel free to create your charts in a way that will catch

Figure 13. Template for Trend Line Charts in the Technical Report

Chart X: Descriptive Title

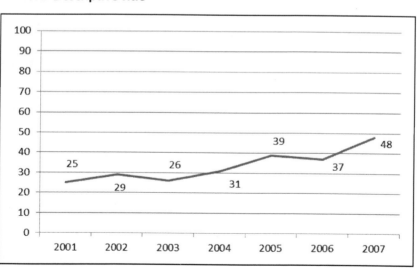

Data Source: If from archival data

the reader's eye. I also prefer to add data labels that give the exact value of each bar or point on a trend line. This provides a more specific description to the chart while illustrating differences among groups or changes over time. I have provided the basics for presenting your findings, but numerous books exist on data presentation. Seek these out if you and your audience desire a more creative look to the report.

Conclusions

Once you have presented your findings, it is time to tell the reader what they mean. Specifically, in this section you will discuss your major findings and answer your research questions. Begin with one or two paragraphs describing what you discovered and any generalizations you can make from the research findings. This is done with text rather than the tables and figures used in your findings section. Try to answer the question: what one or two things do each table or figure actually tell us? Follow these paragraphs with specific answers to your research questions. Feel free to make these answers stand out in an obvious way using italics, bold, or bullet points. Complete this section using:

- Worksheet 15
- Worksheet 21
- Worksheet 22

After answering your research questions, you may choose to further discuss the meaning and implications of these answers. This discussion may point out shortcomings in the research, directions for future needs assessment research in your community, and potential uses for the completed needs assessment.

References

This section should contain specific citations for any literature or publicly available archival data source you utilize in the technical report. For example, you may cite a book that helped you develop a focus group protocol. Unlike a scientific journal article with a literature review, you will likely cite few academic sources. You should, however, cite every publicly available archival data source appearing in the report. The methods section allows other researchers to replicate your process, and part of that replication means finding and accessing publicly available data. References provide this access. Follow the accepted format in your discipline when writing citations. One common style is that of the American Psychological Association (APA). I use it in this workbook.

Appendixes

Finally, there are research elements readers may need or want to see but do not belong in any of the sections above. These are items you append to the technical report because some readers may require the information to better understand the needs assessment. They fall into two categories: data collection instruments and more complicated data analyses. Examples include a focus group protocol, survey instrument, discussion of statistical significance, or demographic tables of survey respondents. In general, the appendixes support your methods and findings sections. When I write technical reports, I always append my survey instrument or data collection protocol. Sometimes I will include discussions of issues like statistical significance or sampling methodology that are beyond the scope of the sections above but serious readers may want to understand more clearly. Of course, it is okay not to have appendixes at all if there is nothing to put in them.

Be aware of two mistakes you can make when selecting items for an appendix. First, you may incorrectly put material in an appendix that belongs in the body of the report. Second, you may fill appendixes with material that no one really wants or needs to see (Pearsall & Cook, 2010). I once reviewed a grant that referred me to an appendix to learn more about the results of a survey of youth. The actual appendix was nearly 100 pages of the printed out database of survey responses—just row after row of numbers. What did the writers want me to do, enter and run the data myself? Again, think of your audience and what they need and want to best understand your needs assessment. Place anything necessary for the research but not appropriate for the above sections in appendixes.

Upon completion, have colleagues read and comment on the technical report, checking for mistakes as well as providing suggestions for improvement. Once you are happy with the product, give it to your needs assessment workgroup for approval. I prefer a formal endorsement from the workgroup to ensure confidence in the product and buy-in from the stakeholders that make up your workgroup. Now with your research complete, research questions answered, and a formal report documenting the process, you are ready to fully use your knowledge and understanding of community need.

FURTHER READINGS

Discussions of report formats exist in most research texts, and you may have examples of reports from your own organization. For a more in-depth dialogue on technical writing and scientific reports, consider reading one of the following texts.

Davis, M., Davis, K., & Dunagan, M. (2012). *Scientific papers and presentations*. New York: Elsevier.
Lindsay, D. (2011). *Scientific writing = thinking in words*. Collingwood, Australia: CSIRO Publishing.
Pearsall, T. E., & Cook K. C. (2010). *The elements of technical writing*. New York: Longman.

For details on in-text references and citations and even more on technical writing style, take a look at the APA publication manual.

American Psychological Association. (2010). *Publication manual*. Washington, D.C.: Author.

Finally, to learn more about clearly and effectively presenting data, read the following from the *Wall Street Journal*.

Wong, M. D. (2010). *The Wall Street Journal: Guide to information graphics: The dos and don'ts of presenting data, facts, and figures*. New York: W.W. Norton & Company.

Using a Comprehensive Needs Assessment

The aim of all this hard work is to use your needs assessment to improve social services, and the premise of this book is that by conducting quality research to better understand your community's needs, you can accomplish this goal. A decade ago, many organizations still planned services and made decisions based upon whatever felt right. Today, in my work with local, state, and federal government agencies as well as not-for-profit groups, I almost never encounter an organization that does not allow data to drive their work. In an age of information, organizations want to know what their community needs and if they are making a difference. You see the impact of this around every corner. My local recreation center recently placed a short survey on the counter asking interested patrons what days and times would be best for rescheduling a triathlon training class. Many commercial websites have spontaneous surveys that "pop up" to gauge the needs of their customers. And I recently conducted a study of parents and participants of a youth theater group just to see if they learned anything from a small musical production.

A myriad of reasons exist to do a needs assessment, and a myriad of ways exist to take advantage of the findings from a needs assessment. This chapter focuses upon four specific and important uses: presenting your findings, writing the needs assessment section of a grant, making decisions, and planning an evaluation.

TASK 12: PUT YOUR NEEDS ASSESSMENT TO GOOD USE

Prior to discussing these uses, let us revisit the strategic planning model discussed in chapter 1. Needs assessment is the first step in a cycle of activity followed by community mobilization, strategic planning, implementation of services, and evaluation. The needs assessment informs each of these. For example, presenting your needs assessment findings can raise awareness and mobilize stakeholders; the data collected during the needs assessment can establish a baseline for your evaluation of community change; and the needs assessment provides much of the information needed to create a solid strategic plan. The next four sections provide specific uses for your needs assessment findings relative to the strategic planning model.

Creating a Presentation

Completing a task as daunting as the research project in this workbook is useless if you do not share it with people. By presenting your findings you build knowledge, raise awareness, and mobilize people to action. Presentations can take the form of simple meetings within your organization, small gatherings of key stakeholders, large demonstrations to the public, or formal testimony in front of a city council or state legislature. In each case your technical report serves as the foundation for your presentation, and in each case you do not want to pass out the technical report. Rather, you should have it with you and create a presentation that summarizes the most important parts of the research.

In graduate school, I was preparing my first presentation at a national conference and my academic chair advised me to spend as little time as possible on my methods and analysis. What attendees really want to know is what you learned, he told me. This is good advice for you as well. A city council, for instance, does not have time to listen to how you created a random sample and has no interest in the equations you used to create confidence intervals. Instead, tell them you used a random sample and move on to the results. Of course, you should mention each of the sections of your technical report, but spend the bulk of your time presenting the findings and conclusion sections of that report.

Depending upon your audience, a public presentation of your needs assessment can take one of two forms: a slide show or a handout. Many people immediately defer to creating a slide show (using a program like Microsoft PowerPoint), but often a simple handout can be quite effective. Use handouts with small groups, in situations where technology may not be available or appropriate, or when you know a slew of other presenters will be using slide shows. In the latter case, your presentation will seem unique. Use slide shows for particularly large audiences, or where such technology is available and expected. Huge advances have been made in available presentation software. The technology exists to pan and zoom your way through a presentation, use video and audio to entertain attendees, and generally wow an audience with your computer abilities. However, fancy technology can also take away from the point of your presentation or backfire if you are not an expert at using it. Nothing detracts from a presentation or undermines a presenter like the failure of technology. You do not want your audience (be it a city council or a huge town hall meeting) to leave remembering the fancy graphics or the presenter's inability to work a computer. Instead, you want them to leave impressed by the answers to your research questions. Also, a major criticism of basic slide shows is that they are simple and very linear, but your needs assessment research itself should be straightforward and linear in its approach.

A handout and a slide show contain the same information. This includes a title based upon the name of the technical report, specific research questions, a description of each data collection method, detailed results, explicit discoveries and generalizations, answers to your research questions, and concluding thoughts about what this all means. Of course, you should use software and a template consistent with your organization.

I used to hate everything about slide show presentations like those given in PowerPoint. However, I recently realized I love giving slide show presentations. I just hate watching other people give them. Programs like PowerPoint have done for our presentation skills what spellcheck has done for our spelling skills—provide a crutch so we no longer work on or care about our own public speaking abilities. Like you, I have witnessed people present from behind a laptop computer, turn and read their slides, or create slides so full of bullet points I would need a magnifying glass to read them. Here are my guidelines for creating effective slide show presentations. First, know your material. If you have to read your slides to understand what you are presenting, then you have not prepared well enough. The slides themselves should provide only landmarks for what you say as well as the most important information from your study. Second, avoid bullet points. This is a problem because slide show software often defaults to slides with bullet points. However, this default leads presenters to begin listing what really should be their speaking notes. A slide show should not be a replacement for speaking notes on a set of note cards. The audience does not want to watch your back as you read your notes. Of course, do turn to look at your presentation whenever you click to the next slide to make sure the technology is working and to lead the gaze of your audience (Weissman, 2013). Third, do not over-animate or over-adorn your slides. You are not a movie director, and your first goal is not to entertain the audience. You can be engaging, amusing, and interesting, but too often presenters include fancy animations or graphics that distract from the message of their presentations. A slide show should serve as supporting material for your presentation. It should illustrate and provide details about your research as you talk through the most important aspects of the needs assessment.

Davis, Davis, and Dunagan (2012) offer further guidance for creating slides. Visual aids should meet five criteria. They should be simple, making one point with limited sub-points. They should be easily understandable to anyone in the audience. They should uniformly match other visual aids and aspects of the presentation. They should be attractive and aesthetically pleasing. And they should be feasible given the time and facilities in which you are presenting. The authors also agree with my assertion that visual aids should not distract from the presentation. They write: "Science is a serious matter. We can certainly be creative and add notes of humor to our presentation, but our communication is essentially to inform and teach. Enjoy the advantages of what technology can do, but when it comes to writing a paper and making a scientific presentation, do not let anything distract from the message" (p. 164). In sum, Davis et al. (2012) believe "a simple slide is the best slide" (p. 170).

Terrific advice about presentations can come from many places, but much comes from the fields of business or politics where presentations can mean the difference between making a sale or leaving empty handed and between winning or losing an election. Venture Capitalist Vinod Khosla follows a five-second rule. If you put up a slide and remove it in only five seconds, can a viewer describe what they saw? If not, your slides are too dense. They should simply and visually support your presentation while making your point instantly (Weissman, 2013). President Obama's 2011 State of the Union address was leaked to the press prior to the actual presentation. As he made his way through the House of Representatives chamber and up to the podium to deliver his presentation, Secretary of

State Hillary Clinton smiled and said "good speech," to which he replied "I don't need to deliver it now, everybody saw it" (Weissman, 2013, p. 87). From this, learn to never pass out your presentation slides before you actually give the presentation. It detracts from the power of your message and distracts the audience from your words. Of course, offer to provide the slides or technical report following the formal presentation, but there is no need to allow audience members to interpret what you mean or what you did prior to hearing you speak. Robbins (1997) tells us when your words and images are combined "maximum impact occurs" (p. 115). She accomplishes this with many of the ideas discussed above. Use as few words as possible. Include only one basic idea per slide. Make sure the idea is easy to understand at a glance.

Similarly, handouts serve as illustrations for your presentation and should reflect the sections of your technical report. The bulk of the information comes from your needs assessment findings. The handout should be easy to read and straightforward. Ideally, a handout covers the front and back of one page of paper, and the more formal the audience, the more likely you should print it in color. Create your handout like you might create a resume: with clear language, proper grammar, relevant information, simple presentation, and an achievement focus. The handout should describe what you did, what you found, and what you accomplished with the research.

Finally, any presentation should end with next steps. This includes what you and your needs assessment workgroup or larger organization might do with the information, but also what you expect from the audience themselves. Why are you presenting this information to them? How do you hope to affect them? What do you hope they will do once they know the results of your needs assessment? The answers to these questions should not appear in the handout or slide show; rather, conclude with next steps as a personal appeal delivered from your mind and heart instead of on a sterile slide or piece of paper.

Writing Grants

Needs assessments are an excellent investment of resources if used to improve grant applications, because a compelling statement of need can lead to increased funding for any social service organization. The second most common mistake among those writing grant proposals (after not following the directions) is not developing a sound statement of need (Bauer, 2007). Moreover, the needs section appears at the beginning of the grant (it also appears at the start of the strategic planning model), and it provides an important first impression to grant reviewers. Your statement of need can say to reviewers "the writers of this grant know what they are doing and their services are definitely needed in their community," or it can say "this community does not necessarily need what they are about to ask for." Of course, you want readers to think the former rather than the latter. Your statement of need also has the potential to make reviewers eager to read about your solutions to community problems.

Miner and Miner (2008) contend your statement of the problem is the single section of your proposal that most influences funding success. From their perspective, this section represents the gap between what currently exists in your community and what might exist in the future, and it should be supported by just the kind of research you completed using this workbook. The statement of need is not just the first thing reviewers read; it is most likely the first thing you write. As such, it sets the tone and voice for your proposal. According to Carlson (1995), "The need statement is at the heart of your entire case for support" (p. 9). She continues: "Preparing the statement of need is a critical part of the proposal, since funders must agree with the organization that the project meets an important need. It is often the compelling need statement that motivates a funder to help" (p. 9). It serves as the hook that sells your proposal.

In the preface, I mentioned a grant proposal for new skates for my local ice speed skating team to a regional foundation that provides money for youth sports activities. The foundation funds projects that keep kids out of trouble by keeping them busy. The opening sentence of the statement of need (and the proposal itself) was, "At 7,200 feet winters are long and opportunities are limited." They jumped on the idea and have funded the small program twice over the past eight years. Demonstration 7 below tells this story in more detail.

In sum, here is a list of very good advice as you sit down to write a statement of need (Carlson & O'Neal-McElrath, 2008; Harris, 2007; Miner & Miner, 2008).

- When appropriate, include or start with an anecdote that humanizes the problem.
- Use data that is easily understandable and represents the extent and frequency of the problem.
- Focus on the needs of the community you serve and not on the needs of your organization.
- Write clearly and avoid jargon.
- Show an obvious relationship between the community's need and your organization's vision and mission.
- Show an obvious relationship between the community's need and the vision and mission of the granting organization.
- Make sure your organization can realistically address the community's need with the funding you apply for.

More specifically, think of your statement of need as a short essay with several very specific paragraphs. Length and detail vary depending upon allowable space, which often increases along with the size of funding. Begin with an opening paragraph that includes a humanizing anecdote and a very specific statement of need. Think of this specific statement as the essay's thesis, and it comes naturally from the detailed answers to your needs assessment research questions. The second paragraph describes the need in more detail. Discuss the frequency and severity of the problem using the findings from your technical report. You cannot include every result, so include only those that clearly and directly relate to the funding proposal. In longer statements of need, it is appropriate to include a table or chart here. For shorter statements of need, simply cite the appropriate data in the written text. The third paragraph answers the question, who needs it? Describe your community and those most affected by the problem using data from the introduction and findings section of your technical report. The fourth paragraph describes the consequences of doing nothing as well as the relevance of the problem to the funder. This is where you describe what might exist in the future should your organization receive funding. The fifth paragraph expands on this idea by showing the relationship of the problem to your organization and briefly describes potential outcomes. The final paragraph summarizes the need and encourages the reviewer to read further to learn about your organization's plan to reach potential outcomes. Of course, alter this outline as required by the specific directions in any request for proposals.

DEMONSTRATION 7: STATEMENT OF NEED FOR NEW ICE SPEED SKATES

Above, I mentioned writing a small grant for a speed skating program which I coach at my local ice rink. I crafted the proposal in collaboration with the city grant writer and under the umbrella of the city Parks and Recreation Department. We submitted the proposal to a foundation that supports (among other activities) youth sports in the Rocky Mountain region and successfully received roughly $9,000 to buy 20 pairs of advanced speed skates and other necessary equipment. Here is a version of our "Issue Statement." It is necessarily short because of page limitations, but it does follow the above outline fairly closely.

> At 7,200 feet winters are long and opportunities are limited. Young people need chances to participate in positive activities that foster confidence, discipline, leadership, and sportsmanship. In the absence of these positive activities, many youth quickly fall into a pattern of problem behaviors. Positive alternatives to problem behaviors are particularly necessary in frontier America, where youth participate in unhealthy activities like underage drinking at much higher rates than the nation as a whole. Programs that provide these positive alternatives need the necessary equipment to build success and sustain opportunities for youth.
>
> The 2011 Youth Risk Behavior Survey has shown that Wyoming youth have significantly higher rates than the nation in several important risk behaviors. These include driving a car after drinking alcohol, carrying a weapon on school property, attempting suicide, having been forced to have sexual intercourse against their will, and smoking cigarettes, using alcohol, or using marijuana before the age of 13.
>
> Laramie, a fairly typical Wyoming community, has attempted to combat some of these problems by providing many positive alternatives for youth. During the long winter, some of the most

important activities now take place at the Community Ice & Events Center. Laramie added short track speed skating to this list in 2004 to target a group of young people who love to ice skate but are not interested in hockey or figure skating. The speed skating program now attracts youth from 3 to 17 years of age as well as adults of any age who live in and around the Laramie area. The program has seen lasting success over the past eight years both in retaining past participants and in recruiting new participants. We have also seen real improvement in the skills of our speed skaters. Many continue to reach personal best times in races, and each year we see records broken in many age groups.

Unfortunately, most of our participants have begun to level off in terms of performance. The initial set of beginner speed skates that helped our program grow (while still in decent working shape) no longer provide our skaters with the necessary equipment to develop their skills and move to the next level. In the past year, we actually saw the loss of some participants and a decrease in speed of others because our beginner skates no longer provide the necessary tools to become a better skater. New advanced speed skates would lead to new participants and give current participants the required equipment and incentive to improve their performance.

The Community Ice & Events Center is in real need of a collection of advanced ice speed skates to continue offering and growing this positive activity for youth. The sections that follow describe how funding for new skates will help the program reach its overarching goal and outcome-based objectives.

Finally, the statement of need lays the foundation for your identified goals and objectives. A well written grant proposal links the specified need to overall benefits (goals) and measurable outcomes and activities (objectives). Writing goals and objectives likely happens in the section following the statement of need, and your proposal will be all the more convincing and effective if you make the logical link between what your community needs and what you hope to accomplish.

Making Decisions

Completion of your comprehensive needs assessment (and the prioritization process described in chapter 9) may have already led to major decisions for your community. This section breaks potential decisions into four related areas in an attempt to further utilize your needs assessment results. These include recommendations, decision analysis, resource allocation, and action planning. Choosing which to pursue and complete provides a terrific opportunity for your needs assessment workgroup to bring closure to their efforts, and making a decision involves promoting future courses of action based upon the answers to your research questions.

Recommendations

If answers to your research questions imply possible choices among two or more alternatives, then simple recommendations are called for (Dunn, 2011). Returning to the example of the food cooperative in exercise 3, the community may have learned the most needed groceries are organic fruits and vegetables as well as locally produced dairy products. The workgroup then makes a recommendation urging the food cooperative to increase amounts of these products when opening their doors to the larger community.

Decision Analysis

However, recommendations might not be simple to make when multiple alternatives with various outcomes exist. For instance, a needs assessment may clearly identify one problem with multiple causes and related solutions. The biggest crime-related problem in our downtown is late-night vandalism to property due to environmental issues like poor lighting and already deteriorating buildings as well as a lack of visible law enforcement. Decision analysis would have the workgroup consider possible outcomes related to three alternative activities: increasing law enforcement, investing in improving the physical environment, or doing nothing. In making their recommendation, the workgroup might also consider the probabilities of success and potential resources and sustainability of each alternative (Patton, Sawicki, & Clark, 2013).

Resource Allocation

The most common use of needs assessment is to shed light on the problem of where an organization should spend its time, energy, and money. In short, how should we allocate our scarce resources? "Advocates argue that one of the major benefits of needs assessment is its potential as a mechanism for making rational choices for resource allocation" (Meenaghan, Kilty, & McNutt, 2009, p. 177). Your comprehensive needs assessment allows decision makers to understand what is most needed in your community. The needs assessment workgroup, then, can recommend resource allocations based upon data rather than upon what feels right or the latest fad problem.

I recently worked with a state very concerned about the problem of methamphetamine use but with only a vague awareness of problems related to alcohol misuse. The needs assessment showed that while 63 percent of all arrests in the state were related to alcohol, less than 2 percent of arrests were related to methamphetamine. Certainly any individual crime involving methamphetamine is a problem, but decision makers quickly learned that more resources needed to be allocated to the problem of alcohol misuse in order to change public health and crime outcomes.

Action Planning

Lastly, and beyond making simple recommendations, you can use your needs assessment findings to create action plans for the future. Data from your needs assessment informs all levels of the planning process (Mitra, 2011), and plans often require or include raising awareness/mobilizing the community (through presentations) and increasing funding (through grant proposal writing). In general, the sections of a strategic plan correspond to the steps in the planning model presented here and in most grant proposals. The strategic plan starts with a statement of need, moves on to goals and objectives, describes strategies for reaching these objectives including community mobilization, and provides for an evaluation of the effort.

Goals are broad based, but objectives must be measurable and specific. This means they describe in detail how identified problems in your needs assessment will change. If your needs assessment found binge drinking among eleventh graders to be 41 percent and among twelfth graders to be 44 percent in 2010, then your objectives would detail exactly how much this will change because of the community plan. For example, "By 2015, binge drinking among eleventh graders in our community will decrease to 35 percent or less." Strategies themselves can include specific services as well as action steps necessary to accomplish these services. Again, decisions about these steps are best when based upon a comprehensive needs assessment. The solid work you did in completing this workbook ultimately allows for a logical and data-based plan.

Planning an Evaluation

While evaluation models vary from goal-free evaluation to fiscal evaluation and beyond (Posavac & Carey, 2011), evaluators generally agree on a definition like the following. "Program evaluation is the systematic collection of information about the activities, characteristics, and results of programs to make judgments about the program, improve or further develop program effectiveness, inform decisions about future programming, and/or increase understanding" (Patton, 2008, p. 39). Program evaluation, whether your unit of change is an individual in an intervention or an entire community, depends upon available data. Collecting data for evaluation is very similar to collecting data for needs assessment, however different its purpose. Therefore, a quality needs assessment provides a wonderful foundation for a quality evaluation of efforts.

Your comprehensive needs assessment offers two very important building blocks for an evaluation. First, as discussed above, needs assessment results allow you to write measurable objectives. These objectives become the hypotheses tested by your evaluation. Consider a needs assessment that found the biggest poverty-related problem in a community to be children going hungry. Indeed, over 13 percent of children under the age of 12 went at least one day a week without food. As a consequence, children living under the poverty level also had significantly poorer school performance than their peers. As a community planned to address these issues, they might write the following objectives.

- By the end of 2015, the percent of children under the age of 12 going at least one day a week without food will decrease from 13 percent to 5 percent or less.

- By the end of 2015, children in our community living under the poverty level will raise their academic performance to match that of their peers.

Remember, understanding need has a lot to do with understanding the gap between what is and what should be (Roth, 1990; Scriven & Roth, 1990). Assume in this case the community has the wherewithal and the resources to try to close the gap. The two outcome-based objectives written above then become the hypotheses of the community's evaluation. While other important evaluation activities may take place, testing whether or not the community met these goals is at the heart of evaluation research.

Second, the needs assessment provides many of the necessary data components for a quality evaluation. This includes baseline measures of a problem. I have occasionally been asked to evaluate a project following its completion, which is impossible if data has not already been collected. Your needs assessment gives an evaluator that good start. In the example of children living under the poverty level having poorer academic performance, two archived data sources must have been utilized—measuring youth in poverty and academic performance. It takes work to find quality measures and the needs assessment documents where the archives are and builds essential relationships to access this data. It also includes methodology for recollecting data and measuring change. Focus group and observational protocols, sampling designs, and survey instruments already exist because of the prior needs assessment. For evaluators, this is an amazing place to begin building an evaluation plan.

As the first step in a rigorous strategic planning model, the comprehensive needs assessment you created here answers questions of need at a community level. I hope this systematic collection of data has done more than answer your research questions. I hope through this process you have built relationships, learned something noteworthy about social science research, and improved your community's understanding and use of data to address social issues. Above all, I hope your community and the people who live there are better off because of your ability to thoroughly and carefully assess what is needed.

FURTHER READINGS

To learn more about creating effective presentations, consider reading these two clever and entertaining books.

Robbins, J. (1997). *High-impact presentations: A multimedia approach.* New York: John Wiley & Sons.

Weissman, J. (2013). *Winning strategies for power presentations: Jerry Weissman delivers lessons from the world's best presenters.* Upper Saddle River, NJ: Pearson Education.

To learn more about successfully writing grants and the statement of need sections of those grants, consider reading one of these helpful how-to books.

Carlson, M., & O'Neal-McElrath, T. (2008). *Winning grants step by step.* San Francisco: Jossey-Bass.

Gitlin, L. N. (2008). *Successful grant writing: Strategies for health and human service professionals.* New York: Springer Publication Company.

Harris, D. C. (2007). *The complete guide to writing effective & award winning grants: Step by step instructions.* Ocala, FL: Atlantic Publishing Group.

Miner, J. T., & Miner, L. E. (2008). *Proposal planning & writing.* Westport, CT: Greenwood Press.

To learn more about program evaluation, including the role of needs assessment in the evaluation process, pick up any evaluation textbook or consider reading one of the following texts.

Brun, C. F. (2005). *A practical guide to social service evaluation.* Chicago: Lyceum Books.

Patton, M. Q. (2008). *Utilization-focused evaluation.* Thousand Oaks, CA: Sage Publications.

Posavac, E. J., & Carey, R. G. (2011). *Program evaluation: Methods and case studies.* Boston: Prentice Hall.

References

Altschuld, J. W., & Witkin, B. R. (2000). *From needs assessment to action: Transforming needs into solution strategies.* Thousand Oaks, CA: Sage Publications.

Arthur, M. W., Hawkins, J. D., Pollard, J. A., Catalano, R. F., & Baglioni, A. J. (2002). Measuring risk and protective factors for substance use, delinquency, and other adolescent problem behaviors: The communities that care youth survey. *Evaluation Review, 26,* 575–601.

Bauer, D. G. (2007). *The "how to" grants manual: Successful grant-seeking techniques for obtaining public and private grants.* Westport, CT: Praeger.

Bronfenbrenner, U., & Morris, P. (1998). The ecology of developmental processes. In Damon, W., and Lerner, R. (Eds.), *Handbook of child psychology,* 5th ed., vol. 1: *Theoretical models of human development.* New York: John Wiley and Sons, Inc.

Carlson, M. (1995). *Winning grants step by step.* San Francisco: Jossey-Bass.

Carlson, M., & O'Neal-McElrath, T. (2008). *Winning grants step by step.* San Francisco: Jossey-Bass.

Corty, E. W. (2007). *Using and interpreting statistics: A practical text for the health, behavioral, and social sciences.* St. Louis, MO: Elsevier.

Creswell, J. W. (2007). *Qualitative inquiry & research design: Choosing among five approaches.* Thousand Oaks, CA: Sage Publications.

Davis, M., Davis, K. J., & Dunagan, M. M. (2012). *Scientific papers and presentations.* Boston: Elsevier.

Dillman, D. (2007) *Mail and Internet surveys: The tailored design method.* Hoboken, NJ: John Wiley & Sons.

Dillman, D. A., Smyth, J. D., & Christian, L. M. (2009). *Internet, mail, and mixed-mode surveys: The tailored design method.* Hoboken, NJ: John Wiley & Sons.

Dunn, W. N. (2011). *Public policy analysis.* Boston: Pearson Education.

Frankfort-Nachmias, C., & Nachmias, D. (2007). *Research methods in the social sciences.* New York: Worth Publishing.

Harris, D. C. (2007). *The complete guide to writing effective & award winning grants: Step by step instructions.* Ocala, FL: Atlantic Publishing Group.

Healey, J. F. (1993). *Statistics: A tool for social research.* Belmont, CA: Wadsworth Publishing Company.

Healey, J. F. (2012). *Statistics: A tool for social research.* Belmont, CA: Wadsworth Publishing Company.

Janis, I. L. (1982). *Groupthink: Psychological studies of policy decisions and fiascoes.* Boston: Houghton Mifflin.

Johnson, J. B., Joslyn, R. A., & Reynolds, H. T. (2001). *Political science research methods.* Washington, DC: Congressional Quarterly Press.

Krueger, R. (1994). *Focus groups: A practical guide for applied research.* Thousand Oaks, CA: Sage Publications.

Krueger, R., & Casey, M. (2009). *Focus groups: A practical guide for applied research.* Thousand Oaks, CA: Sage Publications.

Kvale, S. (1996). *InterViews: An introduction to qualitative research interviewing.* Thousand Oaks, CA: Sage Publications.

Leary, M. R. (2008). *Introduction to behavioral research methods.* Boston: Pearson Education.

Lindsay, D. (2011). *Scientific writing = thinking in words.* Collingwood, Australia: CSIRO Publishing.

Meenaghan, T. M., Kilty, K. M., & McNutt, J. G. (2009). *Social policy analysis and practice.* Chicago: Lyceum Books.

Merriam, S. B. (2002). *Qualitative research in practice: Examples for discussion and analysis.* San Francisco: Jossey-Bass.

Miles, M. B., & Huberman, A. M. (1994). *Qualitative data analysis: An expanded sourcebook.* Thousand Oaks, CA: Sage Publications.

Miles, M. B., Huberman, A. M., & Saldana, J. (2014). *Qualitative data analysis: A methods sourcebook.* Thousand Oaks, CA: Sage Publications.

Miner, J. T., & Miner, L. E. (2008). *Proposal planning & writing.* Westport, CT: Greenwood Press.

Mitra, A. (2011). *Needs assessment: A systematic approach to data collection.* Urbana, IL: Sagamore Publishing.

Osborn, A. F. (1963). *Applied imagination: Principles and procedures of creative problem solving.* New York: Charles Scribner's Sons.

Patton, C. V., Sawicki, D. S., & Clark, J. J. (2013). *Basic methods of policy analysis and planning.* Boston: Pearson.

Patton, M. Q. (2008). *Utilization-focused evaluation.* Thousand Oaks, CA: Sage Publications.

Pearsall, T. E., & Cook, K. C. (2010). *The elements of technical writing.* New York: Longman.

Plested, B. A., Edwards, R. W., & Jumper-Thurman, P. (2006). *Community readiness: A handbook for successful change.* Fort Collins, CO: Tri-Ethnic Center for Prevention Research.

Posavac, E. J., & Carey, R. G. (2011). *Program evaluation: Methods and case studies.* Boston: Prentice Hall.

Robbins, J. (1997). *High impact presentations: A multimedia approach.* New York: John Wiley & Sons.

Roth, J. (1990). Needs and the needs assessment process. *Evaluation Practice, 11,* 141–143.

Salkind, N. J. (2012). *Exploring research.* Upper Saddle River, NJ: Pearson Education.

Scriven, M., & Roth, J. (1990). Special feature: Needs assessment. *Evaluation Practice, 11,* 135–140.

Sork, T. J. (1982). *Determining priorities.* Vancouver, Canada: University of British Columbia.

Stroebe, W., Diehl, M., & Abakoumkin, G. (1992). The illusion of group effectivity. *Personality and Social Psychology Bulletin, 18,* 643–650.

Taylor, S. J., & Bogdan, R. (1998). *Introduction to qualitative research methods.* New York: John Wiley & Sons.

Utts, J. M., & Heckard, R. F. (2004). *Mind on statistics.* Belmont, CA: Thomson Learning.

Wang, C., & Burris, M. A. (1994). Empowerment through photo novella: Portraits of participation. *Health Education & Behavior, 21,* 171–186.

Weissman, J. (2013). *Winning strategies for power presentations: Jerry Weissman delivers lessons from the world's best presenters.* Upper Saddle River, NJ: Pearson Education.

Welch, S., & Comer, J. (2006). *Quantitative methods for public administration: Techniques and applications.* Orlando, FL: Harcourt College Publishers.

Wong, M. D. (2010). *The Wall Street Journal. Guide to information graphics: The dos and don'ts of presenting data, facts, and figures.* New York: W.W. Norton & Company.

Yin, R. K. (2011). *Qualitative research from start to finish.* New York: Guilford Press.

Index

advertising, 67, 125
advisory council, 52
advisory groups, 62
alcohol,
   abuse, 19, 199
   availability and promotion, 30
   misuse, 31, 229
   prevention, 68
   use, 14, 25, 44, 68, 100–102, 199
alcohol-related crime, 199
alcohol-related motor vehicle
   crashes, 199
American Factfinder, 13
American Heritage Center, 33
American history, 60, 160
American Psychological Association
   (APA), 218
amphetamines, 101
answer categories, 105
answer choices, 37, 38
archival data, 33-34, 83–88, 92,
   125–129, 170, 193, 206,
   212–217
archival sources, 83, 125
archives,
   definition of, 32–34
   qualitative, 34–35, 45, 81–88,
   125, 128
   quantitative, 41–46, 87, 125–129

arithmetic average, 38, 44, 155–157,
   166–169, 180, 193
Astrophysical Journal, 201
at-risk populations, 27
at-risk students, 9, 44
audio recording, 26, 60, 70, 72

baseline, 6, 220, 231
bias, 14, 18, 23, 59, 69, 85, 92, 96,
   127
binge drinking, 44, 61, 63, 186,
   192, 199, 230
Black Friday, 32
books, 33, 42, 159, 216, 232, 234
brainstorming, 81–88, 125–127
bureaucracy, 34-35
business, 26, 34–37, 46, 60–61,
   106–107, 146, 222

capacity, 21, 25
Capone, Al, 60
census bureau, 13
census sample, 106–109, 112, 115
census survey, 106
central tendency, 155–157, 160–161,
   166, 175, 179–181
chamber of commerce, 10,
   106–107
changeability, 195–198

charts, 170, 208–209, 212– 216, 225
chewing tobacco, 101
Clinton, Hillary, 223
cigarettes, 36, 41, 81, 93, 101, 125, 149, 181, 199, 226
close-ended questions, 98
coalitions
    campus, 44
    community, 16, 193
    local, 18, 91, 184
    members, 14
    prevention, 18, 30, 109
cocaine, 101
coding, 132, 136–144, 147, 162–169, 172
coding scheme, 162–168, 172
coffee, 27, 56, 72
collaboration, 47, 53, 191, 204, 207, 226
completion rate, 93, 108–109, 111, 114–117
compliance check, 37
computing new variables, 168
confidence intervals, 107, 180–183, 220
consensus, 30, 75, 120, 137, 196–197
consent, 7, 47–49, 54
consumers, 14, 18, 23
consumer groups, 14
convenience sample, 106, 109, 111–112, 116–117
copyright, 207
crimes, drug-related, 153
cultural community, 13

data-based plan, 230
data-driven decisions, 4, 21
data-driven process, 14, 16
data-driven strategic plan, 6
databases
    computer, 162
qualitative, 132-137, 141-143, 146

quantitative, 164–168, 170–175, 179–180, 184, 213
decision-making, 16
demographics
    categories, 13,
    community, 11, 13
    data, 13, 94
    groups, 10, 142
    items, 96
    questions, 96, 102–103, 164
    tables, 217
descriptive statistics, 28, 157, 161, 183
descriptive analysis, 180
digital files, 133–135
digital images, 74, 79
digital photos, 89
digital recorders, 60
digital storytelling, 74, 78, 80
diversity, 14
double-barreled questions, 97
drug-free youth groups, 147, 149
duct tape, 111–112

elevator speech, 192–194, 205, 209
empirical evidence, 40
environment
    campus, 30
    community, 41, 149
    downtown, 137
    natural, 40
    physical, 228
    safe, 28, 83, 125
environmental scan, 30, 32
ethnography, 24
evaluation, 6, 9, 23, 158, 189, 219–220, 229–231

field research, 32
fieldwork, 31
five-point scale, 25, 92–95, 154, 166, 195
five-second rule, 222

focus groups
    defined, 27–28
    examples of, 63
    implementation of, 14, 29–30, 45,
        61–74
    protocol, 70
    purpose of, 28
follow-up questions, 26
follow-up study, 147
frequencies, 170, 175, 213, 215
frequency tables, 183
frequency distributions, 170–177,
        180, 184
frequency tables, 175, 212

generalizability, 109, 157
generalizations
    conclusions and, 149
    definition of, 146, 186
    discoveries and, 131, 146–147,
        186, 192–193, 206, 216, 221
    making of, 21, 35, 107, 113, 146,
        151, 161, 186
geographic community, 10, 13, 33
goal-free evaluation, 230
Goodall, Jane, 30
Google maps, 10
grant writing, 201, 224–229, 232,
        234
graphs, 170, 208, 212–215
grounded theory, 24
groupthink, 196

high-risk drinking, 25, 68, 69
horizontal axis, 215
human subject research, 47
human services, 6, 49, 232, 237
hypotheses, 169, 230, 231
    testing, 183

incentives, 49, 64, 67, 69, 72
indices, 100–102, 168
inferential statistics, 35, 157–158,
        161, 170, 180

institutional review board (IRB),
        46–49
interval/ratio level, 154, 156, 161,
        164, 169, 175, 179
interviews
    conducting, 25–27, 51–61
    examples of, 24–25, 43–44, 147
    interviewee, 25, 54, 56–60
    interviewer, 26, 27, 54, 57–58,
        75
    protocol, 57
    purpose of, 25
inventory, 41, 83, 85–86, 125, 127,
        129
item non-response rate, 105

jimson weed, 3

Khosla, Vinod, 222

label, 132, 136, 154, 162, 164, 206,
        213
Likert scale, 94

margin of error, 108, 181
marijuana, 101, 161, 183, 193, 197,
        213, 226
matrices, 132, 141–143
measurable objectives, 230
measurable outcomes, 227
median, 11–12, 156, 160–161, 175,
        180
methamphetamine, 198, 229
methodological traditions, 24
methodology, 28, 36, 74, 78, 91,
        115, 117, 119, 217, 231
mode, 155, 160–161, 175, 180
moderator, 64, 68–69, 73, 75
monitoring the future, 100
motor vehicle crashes, 157, 159,
        178–179, 195, 199
multimethod approach, 44
mutually exclusive categories, 94,
        96–97, 170, 176

narrowing criteria, 85, 88, 127
needs assessment, definition of, 3–4
needs assessment workgroup
  creating, 13–16
  examples of, 4–5, 18–19, 198–199
  jobs performed by, 52, 58,
    61–64, 83, 125–127, 183–184,
    195–198, 228–229
nominal level, 153–155, 159–164,
  170, 172, 175, 178–181
nonthreatening questions, 29
not-for-profit organizations, 33–34,
  219

Obama, Barack, 222
objectives, 227, 229, 230, 231
observations
  examples of, 138–140
  plan, 80–81, 123
  protocol, 82–83, 124
  qualitative, 30–32, 74–79
  quantitative, 39–41, 117–122
open-ended questions, 26, 28–29,
  32, 37, 55, 71, 131
ordinal level, 153–156, 159,
  161–164, 169–172, 175,
  179–181
organizational community, 10–11,
  13
original research, 32, 35, 41–42, 45,
  81, 199
outcome-based objectives, 227,
  231
outcomes, 147, 225–229

parental consent, 7, 47, 48
participatory observation, 31, 40
passive observation, 31, 80
passive observers, 40, 74, 76, 120
percentage calculation, 177, 180
perception of need, 3
phenomenology, 24
photovoice, 76, 78–79, 89

planning model, 1, 5, 219–220,
  224, 229, 231
prioritization 85–88, 127, 129,
  197–200, 228
prisoners, unethical studies of, 47
professionalism, 58, 207
public health, 3, 18, 24, 30, 116, 229

qualitative data
  analyzing, 131–150
  collecting, 24–35, 51–89
  definition of, 24
  drawing conclusions from,
    146–149
qualitative findings, 132, 211
qualitative interview, 25, 58, 61
qualitative observations, 32, 40, 45,
  74, 80, 82, 119
qualitative research, description of,
  24–25
quantitative analysis, 152, 182–184,
  186, 188
quantitative data
  analyzing, 151–187
  collecting, 35–42, 91–128
  definition of, 35
  drawing conclusions from,
    184–187
quantitative findings, 211
quantitative measures, 35, 38, 42,
  44, 182, 198
quantitative methods, 128, 236
quantitative observations, 39–41,
  46, 74, 117, 119–120, 122–125
quantitative research, description
  of, 35, 36
quantitative survey, 25, 37, 118

random sample, 28, 43, 106–112,
  114, 220
range, computation of, 156–157
rates, computation of, 178–179
ratios, computation of, 177–178

raw data, 153 157, 161, 164, 170, 175, 214
readiness, 24–25, 235
reassembling, 132, 141, 143, 144, 211
recoding, 168, 169
reliability, 100, 105
research questions
    answering, 191–193
    detailing, 17–18
    identifying, 16–17
Reserve Officers Training Corps (ROTC), 27
reviewers, 224
Roosevelt, Theodore, 33

sample population, definition of, 106
sampling frame, 106–118
sampling methodology, 217
scale, 25, 92, 94–95, 98–99, 103, 154, 166, 195, 214
scientific inquiry, 9, 16
scoring, 40, 196–197
semi-structured, 25, 29, 54–56
seven-point scale, 95
social ecological model, 6
social sciences, 3, 7, 24, 231
social service providers, 3, 5, 13, 18, 46, 62, 109, 152, 183, 207
speed skating, 34, 154, 226
stakeholders
    mobilizing, 6, 220
    interviewing, 25–27, 34
State Advisory Council, 52
State Epidemiological Workgroup, 42, 52, 198, 237
statistical analysis, 105, 160, 170, 183–184
statistical significance, 217

statistical techniques, 100
statistics, 13, 28, 35, 116, 151–152, 155–158, 161, 169–170, 179–184, 188, 233–235
strategic planning model, 1, 5–6, 219–220, 224, 231
survey tool, 100
survey data, 92, 181
survey instrument, 92, 100, 117, 209, 217, 231
survey methods, 115–117
survey questions, 7, 93, 97–98, 100–102, 166, 171
survey respondents, 38, 98, 107, 162, 171
survey results, 40, 47, 127, 175
survey template, 7, 49
survey tool, 95–96, 102, 106, 115–117

technical report, 189, 201–217, 220–225
theme questions, 79, 82–83
tobacco, 3, 101, 149, 198–199
triangulation, 43
Tribal Statistical Areas, 13

underserved populations, 19

validity, 100
value labels, 132, 141, 155, 161–164, 168–169, 172, 175, 212–213, 216
variables, 43, 164, 168–170
video recording, 72

Wister, Owen, *The Virginian*, 33
workgroup. *See* needs assessment workgroup

About the Author

Rodney Wambeam is a senior research scientist at the Wyoming Survey and Analysis Center and adjunct professor in the Department of Political Science, both at the University of Wyoming. He has served as health and human services advisor to the governor of Nebraska, on numerous councils and coalitions, and as technical assistance provider to states and communities throughout America. He chairs Wyoming's State Epidemiological Workgroup, and also teaches policy analysis, evaluation, and needs assessment. On a daily basis he uses research to help a variety of organizations and communities better understand their problems and the impact of their work. To learn more about applied community research and to download the worksheets and tools in this book, visit rodneywambeam.com.